The Art of God Incarnate

The Art of God Incarnate

Theology and Image in Christian Tradition
AIDAN NICHOLS O.P.

PAULIST PRESS
New York/Ramsey

First published in Great Britain in 1980
by Darton, Longman & Todd Ltd
89 Lillie Road
London SW6 IUD

©Aidan Nichols 1980

Published in the U.S.A. in 1980
by Paulist Press

Editorial Office:
1865 Broadway
New York, New York
10023

Business Office:
545 Island Rd.
Ramsey, New Jersey
07446

Library of Congress
Catalogue Card Number:
80-81443

ISBN:
0-8091-2300-2

Printed and bound in the United States of America

To

JAMES LOY MACMILLAN

amico dilecto in Christo

Gwela’ i’n sefyll rhwng y myrtwydd
   Wrthrych teilwng o fy mryd,
Er mai o ran yr wy’n adnabod
   Ei fod uwchlaw gwrthrychau’r byd;
      Henffych fore
Y cad ei weled fel y mae.

I see standing among the myrtle trees an object
worthy of my whole mind, although I but partly
know that he is high above all objects in the
world; hail to the morning when I shall see him
as he is.

Ann Griffiths, Hymns

Contents

Illustrations

Grateful thanks are due to the organisations mentioned above for their permission to reproduce the above illustrations.

Abbreviations

Biblical versions cited include the Jerusalem Bible, the Revised Standard Version, and the Authorized Version.

Preface

This book issues from two convictions. Firstly, the value, coherence and distinctiveness of the Christian faith depend on the traditional affirmation of Christians that in the man Jesus of Nazareth God himself lived out a human life. But secondly, given the unique and mysterious nature of this affirmation Christians must keep up a continuous, delicate scrutiny of the old forms in which they set it forth, and a constant, restless search for new ones. Otherwise they will find themselves occupying an island of non-communication, abandoned by their contemporaries as purveyors of the inconceivable and salesmen of the unimaginable.

It may be wondered, however, why so much weight should be attached to such a piece of theology as the incarnation. A moment's attention to the implications of that theology should dispel the puzzlement. The article of the Creed committing the Christian Church to the incarnation amounts to saying that at a certain point in time God began to exist as a human personality and still so exists now. If true, this proposition enables us to hold realistically a vision of the universe so positive as to satisfy our deepest desire for security and meaning. It allows us to shake off the incubus of suspicion that we are displaced persons in a world indifferent to our fate. We can infer from it that we exist because we have been loved into existence, since behind the universe lies a divinely tremendous love for man. God, the Source and Ground of being, so far from showing indifference to man is not only benevolently inclined towards him but loves him so intensely that he willed to take our human nature to his own side in the person of Jesus of Nazareth, thus uniting humanity to himself. If God did become incarnate in a nameable

1

human being, existing as the subject of a human biography, being born, growing up, being tempted, finding his destiny, knowing rejection by friends, acquainted with failure and finally with death itself in order to understand our human condition *per experientiam,*[1] by experience, as St Bernard puts it, then no limit to God's loving involvement with us can be marked out. We may say with Mother Julian of Norwich, All shall be well, and all manner of thing shall be well.[2]

The fact, if it be a fact, that for this reason we want this affirmation of the Creed to be true is not in itself a ground for supposing it to be false. Venal and devious as we may be, human reason is not totally undermined by the vagaries of will and emotion. Intellectual integrity is possible, and moreover it is a moral virtue, by which is meant a part of all decent human living, not just a tool for the advance of scholarship by the few. Hence time and again we ought to test the quality of our theological assertions. We have to ask ourselves whether the truth-claims of incarnational faith are intelligible and plausible. In answering this question we shall not need to set criteria of intelligibility and plausibility so narrowly as to disfranchise that whole metaphorical extension of language whereby we express the deep things of human life. As S. T. Coleridge saw, language as a living organism carrying the meanings of a community cannot be strait-jacketed into a stiffly literal one-to-one correspondence with things. Of its nature it requires us to do much of our thinking by images and to develop our thought by extended analogies.[3] But what is really indispensable in testing the character of theological faith is a convincing range of comparison in ordinary human affairs, such as may throw light on the extraordinary human affair that is the incarnation of God in Christ. This book will suggest that in our experience of art we have such a range of comparison which can help us to make sense of the faith of the Church.

In the opening chapter I indicate why I think the present time is propitious for appealing to this model or extended metaphor of the work of art. This timing is a matter of profound and subtle shifts in the sensibility of our common culture in Western society. There is also a second and subsidiary motive for creating an aesthetic theology today. In the more parochial context of church fellowship in the West, and especially in the Anglican and Reformed

2

traditions of that fellowship, an anxiety over the validity of the old language about incarnation has generated in recent years fundamental doubts about the actuality of the incarnation itself.[4] If we cannot trust our means of expression, we soon come to distrust the content we thought we had to express. The model of the artwork which I am commending has the advantage in this second context of meeting some of the difficulties that theologians have encountered. I hope to show that the model of the artwork can embrace the positive affirmations of anti-incarnationalists about the full humanity and therefore historical contingency of Jesus and about the many-faceted quality of the Christian picture of him, and yet at the same time suggest an ontological foundation, a rooting in the truth of being, for faith in Jesus Christ as the supreme disclosure of the loving purposes of God in history. Too often the request for a 'consistent picture of Christ as truly God and truly man'[5] is made too simplistically, without adequate awareness of the complexity, richness, and depth at which an appropriate consistency would operate. Greater discernment of this complexity in the central perceptions of Christian faith may lead people to see historical and metaphysical knock-down arguments as too shallow by far. If the range of comparison invoked by this book for the revelation of God in Christ draws anyone towards such a deepened perception, it will perhaps have served its purpose.

Debts to many writers in the fields this essay touches will become only too apparent in the reading. It is a duty and a pleasure to thank those with whom I have talked about the subject, especially Father Simon Tugwell of the Order of Preachers, who supervised the lectoral thesis on which this book is based, Dom Illtyd Trethowan, monk of Downside, and Dr Nicholas Gendle. The intuition that there might be a subject here at all derives from the wonderfully all-embracing theological heart of my novice-master, the late Father Geoffrey Preston of the Order of Preachers. Such evidence as appears here for a grasp of the issues of Christian theology must be ascribed to the persistence and patience of another dear and prematurely deceased English Dominican, Father Cornelius Ernst. My interest in the art of the Byzantines was stimulated by a common life with one of its most remarkable interpreters, Father Gervase Mathew. This catena of names may rightly be taken to imply that I see what I have written as issuing *ex ecclesia fratrum*, from a

3

conventual life ordered to contemplation and the preaching of God's Word, however imperfect the product.

House of St Albert the Great,
Edinburgh
the feast of St Benedict 1978

CHAPTER ONE

Setting the Scene

Why might we expect art to be an instructive model for us today in exploring what may be meant by 'the disclosure of God in Christ'? At the very least, it seems odd that Christian theology in modern times has paid such scant attention to the visual arts. In the texture of the Bible lies embedded a metaphor of vital significance for the Scriptures as a whole, that of man made 'in the image of God' and of Jesus in particular as 'the image of the invisible God'. We can hardly expect to grasp the sense and scope of this metaphor unless we have some fairly adequate notion of how art subserves the human search for meaning and truth. For these metaphorical utterances are appealing to nothing other than man's experience of art. Christian tradition also should have alerted us to the significance of art, since after an immense struggle over the legitimacy of making and venerating images in the late patristic period the Christian Church eventually came to see in painting tremendous theological possibilities. An ecumenical Council recognized that art has a virtually sacramental power to bring the intangible within our touching. The icon may display the meaning of the work and person of Jesus Christ, so affirming and exploring the relationships which bind man and nature to God. But how comprehensible and attractive in our own present will this 'range of comparison' prove when a theology modelled on aesthetics has done its work? How likely a candidate is a model drawn from visual art if we are selecting stimuli for fresh advance now in the life of Christian theology? Do we today have attitudes to the visual and the painterly that are propitious and helpful in such a marriage of disciplines?

There can be little doubt that we live now in a highly visual epoch in communication. The public art gallery, the cinema and above all the television set are virtually universal features of edu-

5

cation and recreation from childhood onwards. The power of the visual image as mediated by television in particular has become a crucial debating-point of public ethics in our society, as a spate of anxious analyses bears witness.[1] André Malraux, the man of letters and for a time Minister of culture under President Charles de Gaulle expressed this renaissance of the visual in less ambiguous terms when he turned from literature to film to capture what he called the 'voices of silence'. He declared in a celebrated book and phrase that civilization is not so much a succession of ideologies or philosophies as a 'gallery of images'.[2] And what is more, it is not simply that the visual has surfaced again. There has been an extraordinary shift in the relation between the visual image and its big brother in the media, the written word. It seems that people scarcely expect the word to communicate at all without some reinforcement of its potency by 'visual aid'. Bookshops present façades that look more like exhibitions of pictures than the exteriors of temples of print. This is only a matter of window dressing in the most literal sense of that phrase. Word and image are reverting to a relation Europe has not known since the Middle Ages. At the close of the medieval period typography displaced illuminations. In the eighteenth century there appeared unmistakable signs of a reversal of this revolution and the process which thus emerged quite definitively in the nineteenth century has not ceased to grow in momentum since. First, lithographs and woodcuts were included in the book. Then around the turn of this century the poster image arrived, with Daumier and Doré as its heralds. Finally, in contemporary book production the images on the inside and the outside of a book are frequently an absolutely integral part of what the text has to say.[3]

Paradoxically, at a time of unparalleled theoretical interest in the phenomenon of language, language itself is in crisis. The various scientific approaches that have arisen under the general heading of 'linguistics' share the tell-tale sign of concentrating on the formal structures of the word, rather than bringing out the content that the word is meant to convey. The primary function of language – the expression of what is perceived – goes comparatively neglected. The source of this neglect may be sought in an underground insecurity, seeping through our intellectual tradition, about the power of language to generate and sustain the meanings by which men live. The critic George Steiner has wondered aloud whether we may be

> passing out of an historical era of verbal primacy, out of the classic period of literate expression, into a phase of decayed language, of post-linguistic forms and, perhaps, of partial silence.[4]

He points out that there exist other 'communicative energies' for expressing intellectual and sensuous reality, the visual image and the musical note. He remains undecided, however, as to whether it is really legitimate to give visual art a share in 'the defining mystery of man', a reference to Aristotle's classic formula for man as 'the language-using animal'. Is it possible to re-define man as 'the image-making animal', 'the animal aesthetically aware'? Is the time ripe for such a shift in our sense of the human? A necessarily cursory review of changing attitudes to the arts may illuminate this.

People have brought mightily different sets of expectations to the visual arts. These expectations at one pole consist in seeing art as a window opening on to the really real, a uniquely privileged access to truth. At the other they amount to little more than a request for decorative wall-paper, a coating of occasional pleasurable diversion in life. In Augustan England, for example, it was customary to find in painting no more than a harmless means of preserving the mind from vacuity. Addison voiced the common expectations of the time when he wrote in *The Spectator* that 'the Pleasures of the Imagination' may be deemed worthy of pursuit in so far as they

> do not require such a Bent of Thought as is necessary to our more serious Employments, nor, at the same time, suffer the Mind to sink into that Negligence and Remissness which are apt to accompany our more sensual Delights, but, like a gentle exercise of the Faculties, awaken them from Sloth and Idleness, without putting them upon any Labour or Difficulty.[5]

There could be no sharper contrast with such characteristic eighteenth-century attitudes than what we know of contemporary reactions to the Italian Primitives. The chronicler Georgio Vasari put into the mouth of the Florentine painter Buonamico Cristofani this naive but revealing remark,

> We think of nothing but painting saints, both men and women, on walls and pictures . . . we thereby render men better and more devout, to the great despite of the demons.[6]

In that culture art was approached, in other words, as the visual key to divine grace. It gave entry to the inner power of the Judaeo-Christian story by which men construed the meaning of their existence. The great German critic Erich Auerbach saw this Judaeo-Christian story as proposing a way of interpreting the entire process of the world.[7] The tradition which nurtured the story and its iconographic keys he called 'realistic', in the sense than in it no man and no area of life was held to be untouched by the meaning-bestowing finger of God. Indeed, the unlikely image of a dying man was its central feature. Within this story events were interpreted as *figurae*, figures, of each other. Past events pointed to the future and present events to the past in richly ramifying ways. The whole of history was experienced as itself the *figura* of a hidden reality which was not encompassed by man's time. Auerbach's study of this basic imaginative structure of the Middle Ages led him to the conclusion that it was Dante above all who showed how powerfully and supplely this 'figural principle' could order existence. And yet Dante rendered the immediate actuality of human existence so brilliantly in his poetic work that he unwittingly prepared the downfall of the whole figural way of seeing life. He lent the immediate or empirical aspect of the *figura* a fascination which diverted the sensibility into considering it purely for itself. A kind of logic of the imagination was spawned which developed its own grounding premiss until it reached the dogmatic positivism of the mid-nineteenth century, the cult of hard facts. For it is what we find that we can do with our imagination, as much as or more than what we can do with our concepts, that determines what we can count as 'the real'. Human life came to be seen as totally embedded within the objective system of historical circumstance, unrelated to any reality that transcends the temporal.

The picture of existence as an enormous molecular combination of atomic hard facts arouses, once entertained, quite proper philo-

8

sophical doubts. More important, perhaps, is the realization that on this view of the real the human spirit will founder in shipwreck, and that those who care publicly for the life of the spirit, the artist, the poet and the priest, must eventually rebel against it. If the real be atoms of hard fact then man stands over against a self-enclosed and unresponsive world. He peers at the world as a spectator in a box before the theatre arch. Before such a world there can be but two reactions. Either we content ourselves with reproducing its hard facts as on a negative, as did those Victorian thinkers who tried to reconstruct human ethical values by reference to the laws of matter. Or, in despair, we foist on to this world some fantasy of our own which tells us about nothing save the dreams of our own ego. For the world does not carry within itself the power and radiance of significant presence. When we encounter it we do not 'see into' anything.[8]

> A heap of broken images, where the sun beats,
> And the dead tree gives no shelter, the cricket no relief;
> And the dry stone no sound of water.[9]

No pattern of meaning emerges between ourselves and the rest of existence if we accept the aesthetic and metaphysic of positivism. We are, in particular, systematically discouraged in the life of the imagination and the life of reason, as positivism presents them, from all alertness to signals of transcendence in our experience.

Around the turn of the century the crisis which T. S. Eliot registered in the passage of *The Waste Land* I have quoted was lived through and resolved by a group of quite seminal artistic figures in the realm of painting. In so doing these men brought once again within our imaginative reach an approach to the painterly image as a healing and transforming disclosure of a world which is already a sacrament of presence. This crisis and its resolution took place in the crucial shift from Impressionist to post-Impressionist art. If we wanted to label this turning-point we might call it 'the Impressionist crisis in the epistemology of painting'. It is important enough to delay us for a moment. Claude Monet, perhaps the purest Impressionist of the school, once spoke of his 'constant commerce with the external world'. By this description Monet implicated himself in the positivist fallacy. Like so many of his contemporaries

9

he could not see – and the English idiom for intellectual apprehension is especially appropriate here – that the relation of subject and object proper in the natural sciences might be improper if we looked by means of it for a total vision of the world. Monet, like Pissarro and Seurat, sent himself to school with the natural scientists partly through a genuine fascination with optics but partly through an uncritical acceptance of the Pan-Scientism of the age. At the time the Gobelin tapestry works had acquired a team of physicists and chemists to assist in the restoration of fabrics, and the Impressionists hit upon the notion that they might find in the research at the Gobelin the answers to their problems as artists. What if the brilliance of light could be reconstructed on canvas by attention to the prismatic colours of which it is composed?[10] What if the photograph, newly invented, could serve as a basis for a novel, thoroughly realistic, composition in painting? This rigorous concentration on surface appearance, scientific in its rhetoric, produced such works as Monet's *Boulevard des Capucins*. Its representation of tiny pedestrians in a street-scene reproduces exactly the effects found in contemporary photography. Now there is no incompatibility between exact and scientific study of the techniques of brush and pen used in art and the conviction that art has vital, even visionary, meanings to convey.[11] But did the Impressionists at the height of their self-confidence make any such distinction? It seems not. Their failure to do so precipitated an internal crisis in the school which had implications beyond their own work and beyond the tradition of art itself. Cézanne was to write later of Monet, 'He is only an eye, but a magnificent eye'. It is that 'only' which is revealing. Is Monet's *Rouen Cathedral*, a conception existing in a number of canvases painted in different lights, not strictly a conception at all but merely the painterly equivalent of that 'buzzing, blooming confusion' which the philosophical psychologist William James took the unformed deliverances of the human senses to consist in? A certain anxiety on the subject comes to expression in this confession of Monet's:

> Colour is my day-long obsession, joy and torment. To such an extent indeed that one day, finding myself at the death-bed of a woman who had been and still was very dear to me, I caught myself focusing on her temples and automatically analysing the

succession of appropriately graded colours which death was imposing on her motionless face. There were blue, yellow, grey tones – tones I cannot describe. That was the point I had reached.

About the mid-60s Monet and other artists around him began to paint a number of scenes reflected in water, a development which one major student of Impressionism has seized on as highly significant. 'Reflections became a means of shaking off the world assembled by memory in favour of a world perceived momentarily by the senses.'[12] In *The River* Monet's boats and people are hardly more than spots of colour. Human meanings are put under threat by this dispassionate objectivity. It is worthwhile comparing Millet's portrayal of the hardships of peasant life in the pre-Impressionist *L'Arrivée au Barbizon* with the utterly dispassionate and unevaluative *Peasant Woman with a Donkey* by Pissarro. This last canvas though painted by an artist of strong social reforming convictions is wholly uninformed by any trace of social compassion. Baudelaire responded by a broadside against the assimilation of art to the craft of the camera. 'In this silly cult of nature unpurified, unexplained by imagination', he wrote, 'I see the evidence of a general decline.'[13] More importantly, the hollowness of the approach to the world and to art which drew Baudelaire's strictures was exposed in the actual work of a series of artists who broke with that cult and in so doing transformed the range of artistic attitudes and perceptions open to us in our culture. Cézanne, Gauguin, and Van Gogh all saw that a passive attitude to the object was not good enough. On pain of death from inanition art must disclose what is humanly significant, must possess the character of a *sign*. Artworks must be revelatory after their own fashion, vehicles of presence.

Cézanne penetrated into the structural forms of nature in canvases like his study, *Sainte-Victoire seen from the Lauves*. His art constrains you to say that the world is a place in which lies implicit the kind of transcendent order and harmony apprehended by the painter.[14] Gauguin made a synthesis of line, colour, form and image to evoke an all-pervasive poetry and mystery. A work like his *Vision after the Sermon* shows art struggling to be free from the notion that pictorial images are mirror-like reflections of the outside world. Instead, that world is to generate in art symbols that work upon

11

the interior life of man and evoke a new world of meaning for him, disclosing further reaches of the real through the vista it offers. In Gauguin's case such a fresh world of meaning, 'transcendent' in relation to other 'worlds' of less plenitude, came to supreme expression in *Te Rereioa*, his evocation of the paradisal Age of Gold.[15] Lastly, in Van Gogh there appeared in colour and line a tragic vision of life comparable in its power to that of the Attic tragedies or of *Lear*. In *Crows over the Wheatfield*, a work from the last month of his life, the black birds, the wheat ready for the harvest and the ominous sky suggest the inevitability of loss and waste. But three paths organizing the picture space in the form of a cross hint at a transcendent resolution, glimpsed beyond suffering. 'The unseen head of the painter-Christ lies at the convergence of the horizontal and vertical axis outside the painting, looking to heaven.'[16]

With the work of these men a new approach to art, therefore, and with that a new approach to the real became possible. The late Sir Herbert Read saw the guiding thread for the future in Klee's dictum that the purpose of art 'is not to reflect the visible but to make visible'. Similarly, Max Beckmann borrowed from the Jewish Kabbala a programmatic statement of the service that art, at its finest, can do for us: 'To get hold of the invisible, penetrate as deeply as possible into the visible'. It seems that our twentieth century is not the worst time for refreshing theology by attention to art. If the distinctive character of aesthetic reality and communication can throw light at all on the nature and possibility of revelation we should be well enough prepared by the life of our own culture for testing the merits of the model of the artwork in Christian theology.

12

CHAPTER TWO

The Images of Israel

The comparison between the artistic image and revelation in the theological sense was first instituted in the Bible itself. We shall now trace the outlines of the primary scriptural metaphor from which the model of the artwork can be drawn, man created 'in the image of God'. Christian theology, if it is to be recognized as such, must show its coherence with the biblical text, the privileged witness in the record of God's self-disclosure. What, then, is the original context of this metaphor in the Scriptures and in the life of the community of Israel which the Scriptures attest?

Our chief task is to look at the text of Genesis 1 in which the metaphor is embedded, and to try and recover the theology that lies behind it in the work of the Priestly School, that remarkable movement of the Baylonian Exile. We shall need to assess too the presuppositions in the distinctively Israelite background that made the emergence of this striking metaphor possible and intelligible. It is clear that the metaphor has no Old Testament background if by 'background' we mean a history of use of the idea of effigy-making and painting to speak of the relationship of God and man. But we are certainly at liberty to ask what aspects of Israelite thought and experience help to show how this piece of the Priestly theology came to be adopted by an Israelite writer. The work of locating a text in terms of its sources is important enough. Even more crucial and intriguing for the student of the Bible is evaluating the role of the text in its actual use in Israel, as part of the texture of distinctively Israelite faith and experience.

Two notable facets of Old Testament faith should attact our attention. Firstly there is what may be called the negative presupposition of the metaphor which can be found in the aniconicism of classical Yahwism. Images are conspicuous by their absence in the normative form of the religion of Yahweh, God of Israel. Since God may not be directly imaged in the cult there are no obvious candidates for the title 'image of God'. The second and positive presupposition of the metaphor consists in a second pertinent aspect of Hebrew culture, the theomorphism of the Israelite view of man. Yahweh can in some sense be seen in Israel, by means of the 'form' of the existence of his servants the prophets, whom he moulds by his gracious hand. Both of these facets lie present in the implicit structure of the Priestly work. It outlines a cult where Yahweh is nowhere iconically represented, and it teaches the imagehood of God in man while consistently avoiding anthropomorphic language about God. If we keep these defining characteristics of the Priestly writing steadily in our view it should occur to us that the image metaphor is seen right way up when it is approached from the theomorphic anthropology of Israel rather than from an anthropomorphic theology in Israel.[1] It is such an account of man as capable of being graced by God to express God that points, indeed, to the unity of the Scriptures, where the New Testament stands as the fulfilment of the Old.[2]

Man and the Priestly School

The account of creation in Genesis 1 belongs to that strand in the text of the Pentateuch which scholars trace to the Priestly School, a group of 'traditionists' (professional rememberers of religious tradition), editors, and theological writers working in the Exile or shortly afterwards to lay down a ground-plan for a revived Israel after the cataclysm. It must be admitted that this sounds a suspiciously donnish conception of the origins of an ancient religious text. Scholars of the Scandinavian School in particular have insisted as a counter-balance that the growth of the Pentateuch was no scissors-and-paste affair in some Ancient Near Eastern version of an academic's study. The Pentateuchal materials underwent constant modification as they were lived and prayed with in the oral tradition of Israelite worship.[3] Yet the stylistic quality of Genesis 1 is peculiar, pointing us to a common location for this text and for a series of others betraying the preoccupations and theological convictions of a distinct group of men. Contrasted with the alternative account of creation in Genesis 2 it is notably terse, lacking in

14

conscious artistry and ordered to rather rigorously doctrinal teaching. It shows that focus on God's will and word, his judgements, commands, and regulations, which may at once be associated with the scribal work of the Israelite priesthood.[4]

The Priestly Theology takes the form of a special reading of the history and traditions of the people of Israel. It is itself cast as a history. The clue to its aims may be found in the extensive regulations about Israel's faith and worship which crop up at various points in this *sepher tol'doth*, the 'Book of Generations'. These 'legal' sections earned for the Priestly writing the title of the 'Priestly Code', but that is a misnomer. The heart of the document lies not in law but in theology, in a teaching about how the holiness of God is communicated to Israel. This divine holiness spilling over into the life of men is first and foremost on the Priestly view the gift of God; but on the basis of the capacities bestowed in that gift there comes the command to express in all the departments of life the privilege of this unique relation to God. The writers have taken over the pattern of a much older text, the 'Holiness Code' of Leviticus 17–26. This has the recurring imperative refrain, 'You shall be holy, for I, your God, am holy.' The Priestly history writes of the past only to look more clear-sightedly to the future. Its aim is to re-fashion the life and worship of Israel, bringing down the barriers to the return of Yahweh's presence so that Israel might be once more and in the fullest sense the people of God. That divine presence is spoken of by the Priests as the sending of God's 'Glory' to dwell with his people. By this concept of the glory of God setting up camp with men two convictions could find voice. First, God is not present in the midst of Israel by an exhaustive donation of himself to them, *volens nolens*. This error was the root of the spiritual complacency which the pre-exilic prophets and especially Jeremiah had castigated. God does not cease to be the transcendent Lord of the universe who dwells 'in heaven'. He is not tied down but utterly and sovereignly free, even though he commits himself to his people out of an unconditional will to share a life with them as their God. Second, the notion of glory carries the insistence of the Priestly writers that the worship of the Israelite cultus has been given to the people as an act of God's grace. It is not something man does to propitiate God. The 'tabernacling' of God in his worshipping community is in its every aspect an initiative of grace.[5]

15

We must now turn to the role of the text that contains our metaphor in all this. An impressive passage like Genesis 1, with its weighty, liturgical-sounding Hebrew, can hardly be dismissed as a more or less insignificant prologue. If we bear in mind that in the history the prerogatives of Adam pass down through Seth to Abraham, the first man being also the first Israelite, we shall see that the creation account lays down in some way the primordial condition of possibility for the presence of the divine glory in the Israelite community. It is because of a special relationship established by God in creating man that the rest of the story may follow as it does. Adam is, as the rabbinic writers later present him, the first patriarch. Because of this special relationship human life, as the highpoint of a pyramid-shaped cosmos where the base of creation reaches up and narrows to its apex, can be the locus for a divine self-revelation and a divine presence in the history of that beloved Israel who springs from the loins of Adam.

Yet the theme of the image is curiously isolated in the Priestly writing. It recurs in the account of Noah's covenant in Genesis 9 as an explanatory note added to a law making murder a capital offence. 'Whoever sheds man's blood, by man shall his blood be shed, for God made man in his own image'.[6] Yet it can hardly be claimed that the theme is in any explicit way a controlling one in the Priestly work. It is this odd combination of relative isolation with a highly strategic position that makes the metaphor of the image such a controverted but vital subject of Old Testament study.[7]

At this point we may well remind ourselves of the text:

> And God said, Let us make man in our image, after our likeness: and let them have dominion over the fish of the sea, and over the fowl of the air, . . . and over every creeping thing that creepeth upon the earth. So God created man in his own image, in the image of God created he him; male and female created he them. And God blessed them, and God said unto them, Be fruitful and multiply, and replenish the earth, and subdue it: and have dominion over the fish of the sea, and over the fowl of the air, and over every living thing that moveth upon the earth.[8]

This modest length of rather repetitive and incantatory Hebrew has called forth a torrent of exegetical ink. Most exegetes cannot drag themselves away from the passage until they have ascertained, to their own satisfaction at least, which aspect of man it is that the Priestly writer has in mind when he sees him as mirroring God.[9] The bewildering array of 'solutions' indicates that there is something wrong with the approach. A survey of interpretations of the chapter in exegetical history would bring out the inveterate tendency of the commentators to read their own favoured anthropology into it. This is as true of contemporary Old Testament scholars as of the early Christian Apologists and Fathers.[10] It is better to begin from two incontestable data which we have already acquired in our study of the overall structure of the Priestly writing. First, it is clear that man is a disclosure of God in the cosmos, the 'icon of God in the temple of the world'. Second, this is a condition of possibility for the blessing of the divine presence in Israel. From this base we may proceed to a rather closer examination of the language in which the metaphor is couched.

Semitic scholars tell us that *selem*, image, is related to a variety of words whose setting in life seems to be that of sculpting or painting. These include the Syriac *sallem*, to form; the Aramaic *sallem*, to furnish with sculpture, and the later Hebrew *sillem*, to depict. It cannot be absolutely certain that our word, *selem*, does not lean on some verbal root now lost to us but shared by these later cognates, a root which we might need in order to find what linguists call its 'transparency' or capacity to suggest to its user the reason the word carries the meaning it does. It is highly likely, however, that such a lost root would take us back by another track to the very ancient Akkadian verb *salama* or *zalama*, to cut or shape. This is a verb whose noun form is *salmu*, effigy or painting.[11] A German scholar appears to have been the first to fill out the cultic background of this word, against the backcloth of Ancient Near Eastern civilization, in an article published during the First World War.[12] His enquiry opens up a remarkably interesting world to our inspection.

The *salmu* of the god is the cultic artwork which bears his likeness, and is regarded as his manifestation and quasi-living incarnation. We can draw out the religious context of the word from older Sumerian as well as neo-Babylonian material contemporary

17

with the Priestly School, since religious forms in the cultures of the Tigris and Euphrates valleys show very marked continuity of significance.[13] In Sumerian thought man is created in order to serve the gods. It was, therefore, of the highest importance that his service should be carried out according to the right rules of an exact and craftsmanlike liturgy. Modern excavation has uncovered a large number of the temples in and from which liturgies were enacted. Common to them all is an inner room with a niche for the image of the god and a sacrificial altar. The space of this central room is a confined one, because the temple was not in the first place an arena for religious ceremonies but the dwelling-place of the god where he was present in a special way among men. The general public had no right of access to the room where the image stood, although in a number of cases the figure might be visible through a series of angled doorways. On 10 Nisan, the festival of Akitu, however, this normal state of affairs was disrupted. The king entered the shrine and 'taking the hand' of Marduk, the chief and increasingly the exclusive name for God, bore the image in a triumphant progress around the city of Babylon to a house specially appointed to receive it. There then took place a liturgy in which Marduk through his image entered into a ritual combat with Tiamat, the personification of the forces of chaos, destruction and cosmic death. With Marduk's victory these powers were hurled back, so that men could begin a new year in peace and under the divine blessing.[14] It is fascinating, although of course conjectural, to speculate how Israelite priests in exile might have moved among the polyglot crowd that thronged the streets of the imperial capital on such festivals. Second Isaiah in the same period seems to show a first-hand knowledge of Babylonian religion. The Priestly creation account may well have been written for a Jewish version of the Babylonian New Year festival as the liturgical *pièce de résistance* for the start of the Jewish year. But whatever the routes the influence travelled, Genesis 1 depends beyond doubt on these symbolic motifs of pagan ritual and myth.

To the student of comparative religion there is little in the Babylonian picture of belief and worship to arouse surprise. As Gerardus van der Leuuw has written, 'The sacred must possess a form . . . it must "take place".[16] Only what stands before our eyes as image, form, figure, has meaning for us, only that confronts us as power.

Therefore, a primitive man who treats an image as the reality it represents is not simply in error but in sin.[17] In ancient Israel there was a widespread realization of how easy, but how deeply wrong, such transgression would be. Precisely this mark of the Hebrew consciousness makes the Priests' use of a metaphor drawn from the cultic artwork into the daring novelty that it is. They give to *man* the power of divine disclosure attached in a related but competitive and hostile pagan culture to the image of the god. It was an extraordinarily bold step to take, especially for writers with the high doctrine of God's transcendence that the Priestly School possessed. Their handling of the traditions about the Exodus shows that it was otherwise unthinkable for them that Yahweh should be visible to the eyes of sinful men. They guarded their innovation by a lexical hedge, choosing a word comparatively free from association with the traditional vetoes on idolatry, bypassing words like *pesel, masseka, semel, t'muna*, and qualifying *selem* itself with the rather weaker *d'mut*, likeness. But the novelty and the courage remain.

What purpose were these qualities set to serve? Professor James Barr, a Scottish Old Testament scholar, has taken up a fresh angle of vision on the whole subject by way of comparing the Priestly work with the nearly contemporary oracles of Second Isaiah.[18] There are marked similarities between the two: the same stress on creation, the same universality of outlook, the same emphatic monotheism and the same assurance of the incomparability of the God of Israel. Second Isaiah, however, created a major problem for theological thought. As Barr points out, he pressed home his opposition to graven images so strenuously and denied so emphatically any analogy to God from the side of the world ('To whom then will you compare me, that I should be like him? says the Holy One'[19]) as to leave it quite doubtful how God is disclosed in his creation at all. Second Isaiah had no need to tease out an answer to this question for the *genre* of his writing is far removed from an ordered account of the world and of man. But the Priests in their very different task could scarcely avoid it. We may see the metaphor of the image in Genesis 1 as their response to the question, perhaps evoked by the scroll of Isaiah, Is there anything in the world which stands in relation to God as the ground of possibility for that self-disclosure which our traditions about his presence assume? Their

19

answer is, Indeed yes, man himself, for God has made him 'in his image'.

The anti-iconic commandments

For classical Yahwism if not for all men and places in ancient Israel the making of cult-images of Yahweh was utterly out of character with what was believed about God's being and will. What forms did the resultant hostility take, and what theological factors may be said to underlie it?

The Old Testament is frequently to be found conducting a struggle in these matters on two fronts, and it is important to distinguish them in following the battle. First of all, there are texts concerned with *pagan* cultus that betray an increasingly sharp hostility to iconic pagan worship in the nations around Israel. We shall be right to correlate this with a change in the pattern of faith in Israel. The conviction that the tribes who had been the object of Yahweh's gracious action in being chosen, saved from their enemies at the Sea of Reeds and brought into the Land of Palestine must worship no other God than Yahweh (Mosaic Yahwism), ripened into the faith that Yahweh himself is the sole and exhaustive subject of the divine (the prophetic Yahwism of the Exile and the Judaism that succeeded it). The veneration of images by the pagans on this later view is futile, for the pagan deities are mere air, 'vanity', false imagination.[20] The taunt that attributes to the pagan worshipper a sense of his god as in every respect co-terminous with the physical object before him contains a very large element of caricature. By stressing the physicality of the cult-image rather than the perceptual or aesthetic 'object' the pagan man contemplates (this chunk of wood daubed, this mass of stone cut about) these texts remind one of nothing so strongly as of the sophisticated rationalist critique of images in the pagan world of Greece and Rome. Horace, for instance, must have withdrawn himself from the still potent experience of approaching the divine by images in his culture when he mocked in the *Satires*,

Once I was a fig-tree, good-for-nothing wood, when the craftsman, after hesitating a while whether to make me a stool or a priapus, decided for the god.[21]

It has been pointed out that, within the rationality of pagan religion such arguments – that the image is necessarily futile because it is material and made by human hands – are quite inconclusive.[22] For the worshipper the past history of the material composing the image no more proves that it is not now the vehicle of divine grace than the past history of my body proves it is not now animate. The crucial question is rather the authenticity of the rites deemed to charge the image with the presence and power of the Holy. Israel's conviction, as we find it in Second Isaiah, the Letter of Jeremiah and the book of Wisdom is that no such authentication had been given to any religious ways into the divine presence other than that granted by sheer grace to Israel herself.

We come closer to the heart of Israelite aniconicism when we consider the texts of the biblical prohibitions on images of Yahweh himself. The second of the Ten Commandments in Exodus 20 is the first text that should detain us. While the form and covenant-setting of these Commandments could perfectly well belong to the Mosaic age, most commentators believe that the text has been modified by a process of re-application to the changing conditions of Israel's life. This raises the possibility that the ban on images belongs to a later time than Moses', perhaps to the period of sustained contact between a sophisticated and urbanized Israelite population and the culture of Canaan in Palestine and the Mediterranean littoral towns which we can date to the time of the separate monarchies in Israel and Judah. Did the ban on images enter then as a way of securing the purity of Yahwistic faith against an uncontrolled and rampant syncretism?

In the oldest strata of the book of Judges we can just discern, beneath the fortunately unsystematic editorial attempts of the Deuteronomic historian, the signs of an iconic, image-using, Yahwism in the pre-monarchic period. The stories in question belong to a period when it was becoming clear that faith in Yahweh and the religion of the cosmic death and rebirth of life and fertility that centred on the Canaanite saviour-deity Ba'al could not simply be combined. The hero Gideon, for example, bears the name Jerubba'al, 'May Ba'al strive for (the one who bears his name)',

21

but a popular etymology added to the biblical source deftly inverts this meaning into 'Ba'al must plead against him'. Gideon breaks decisively with Ba'al worship, tearing down his altar and sacred tree-pillar. But he goes on to use the gold rings of his troops' battle-spoil to make for Yahweh an *ephod* which he then set up in his own city of Ophrah.[23] Similarly, in an addition to the Book of great antiquity, Micah takes for his priest a Levite, a custodian of the Mosaic tradition, but erects a silver *ephod* on Mount Ephraim where he had a 'house of God'.[24] Old material from Assyria and Ugarit suggests that the *ephod* is identical in form and function with the Greek *ependytes*, a cloak or mantle for an image, usually star-studded because of the symbolism of the starry firmament as the garment of the gods.[25] The Yahwism of the time of the Judges could express itself, it seems, in art-works representing the heavenly glory of the invisible God of Israel. In the Jacob-cyle of sagas in the book of Genesis we also hear of images known as *teraphim*; and these were probably the images of the 'God of the father', the guardian Lord of the patriarchal group who had no name save that of his relation with his worshippers.[26] It is likely that these images in the patriarchal religion which preceded the explosion of Mosaic Yahwism in the events of the Conquest were images such as a man could carry with him when he was unable to discharge his cultic obligations at the sanctuaries where the God of the fathers was worshipped by Hebrew groups already domiciled in Palestine before the great invasion from the south. These stories were passed down by a Judaean writer well acquainted with the Mosaic tradition and known as the Yahwist. Is Mosaic aniconicism, therefore, a figment of the imagination of later writers bemused by the onslaught of the prophets against the images under the monarchies? Is it the case, perhaps, that people *created* this supposed piece of religious history by saying to themselves that since such-and-such was recognized as God's will now, why, it must always have been done so? Certainly, the evidence that there were iconic Yahwists under the Judges, and that sagas of iconic patriarchal figures could be passed down by later Yahwists without a blush, is part of the solid data of Old Testament study. But no data are self-interpreting. The evidence in question is not necessarily any kind of evidence that the *official* cult of Yahwism was ever other than aniconic, except in times of blatant syncretism and corruption.

For confirmation on the point we can turn to the book of Deuteronomy. Embedded within that oratorical tract for reforming Israel there is a much older text known as the Shechemite Dodecalogue. It contains the most ancient formulation of a total ban on images.[27] This series of curses was probably pronounced over the community at the climax of a pilgrimage festival. It implies that a pilgrim may well have an image of Yahweh set up at home, making his private cult in its presence. The veto of the curse gives voice to the practice and convictions of the priesthood at the official sanctuary. For them, Yahweh's worship is imageless; accordingly, they make the acceptance of aniconicism a condition of entry into the sanctuary. In the Decalogue of Exodus 20 the ban is drafted with reference to the worship of other gods than Yahweh, as that is forbidden in the first commandment of the ten. It forbids the representation of Yahweh in an image belonging to *another* deity, and is, therefore, a more nuanced and ambiguous affair than its counterpart in Deuteronomy. It has been suggested that the veto as couched in this more limited form belongs to a much later time, when Yahweh was being worshipped in forms and concepts employed in the cult of Ba'al, the time of Hosea, say, in the eighth century.[28] But it is just as possible, surely, that the emphatic stress on the wrongness of imaging Yahweh in symbols drawn from 'the heavens above, the earth beneath and the waters below the earth' is directed against the theriomorphic gods of Egypt. Indeed it is more likely, for a universal veto on animal forms would be excessively expansive if the only enemy in sight were the bull-images of Yahweh whose artists had borrowed the symbolism of the mighty strength of Ba'al. *A priori*, it seems likely that a more limited veto on images than the one contained in Deuteronomy and its source would be earlier, not later. It would be easy to tighten up such vetos, not so easy to relax them. This means that the aniconic ban in the Ten Commandments can be no later than the last years in the life of the northern kingdom, the time when the bull-images on the throne of the invisible Yahweh at shrines in Dan and Bethel first came under attack. While we cannot be certain, then, that the religion of Moses himself was aniconic, there is a strong possibility that the Second Commandment reflects his teaching and is a ban on the use of motifs and images drawn from the cultic art of Egypt. What we can be sure of is that the priesthood of the official sanc-

23

tuaries in Israel, men entrusted with the preservation and transmission of Mosaic tradition, did teach and practice total aniconicism. Some of their number recalled this fact when writing Deuteronomy, in much anguish over the deviant liturgical art of the northern kingdom in its declining years. By placing the speeches in Deuteronomy on the lips of Moses himself they ensured that such aniconicism would be binding on Israel in the future.

What was the theological rationale of this veto? The Deuteronomist himself speaks of it in terms of the Sinai revelation.

> Then the Lord spoke to you out of the midst of the fire; you heard the sound of words but saw no form; there was only a voice.[29]

Israel did not see God on Sinai. She merely heard the echo of his voice in the thunderstorm, and in the prophetic ear of Moses. Even if this is 'only a substantiation from history and not an explanation',[30] it is certainly a ground for tracing the assault on images to a desire to protect God's transcendence. The selection of images is God's affair, not man's. In the narrative of the Sinai events in the book of Exodus the editor, after the recital of the Ten Words containing the Mosaic ban, sets the scene for the further commands of the Book of the Covenant by affirming that this God with whom the children of Israel have to do dwells in 'the thick darkness'.[31] Yahweh does not show himself in nature and in history inevitably and ineluctably, as though these were modes of his being. He is sovereignly transcendent of them, however powerful the sway he holds in this world. He is not at Israel's command, but gives himself freely, disclosing himself in the way that he, not man, chooses. This, at least, is how a central theological writer in Israel interpreted her aniconism. The Deuteronomist's view throws much light on that general assault on images among the nations which we have noted and which became in the inter-testamental period a commonplace in apology for the truth of Judaism.

Vladimir Lossky, like the Priestly writer a theologian in exile, but this time in the Russian Christian Diaspora of the twentieth century, commented on Israel's refusal of the image:

> If he (the Lord of Israel) excludes images and condemns the

curiosity of those who would pry into his transcendent nature it is because the initiative of revelation belongs to him alone in the history of the people which he has chosen.[32]

But, we shall now go on to argue, the divine mastery of the 'form' of the existence of 'his servants the prophets' enables particular privileged Yahwists to be seen as expressing in their persons and on their faces the meaning God wishes to communicate to his people. Through the experience of the prophetic servants of God as signs of God's action and presence to his people a structure of faith was created in Israel which the Priestly work succeeded in making explicit. Man himself can be recognized now as living 'in the divine image' without fear of misunderstanding.

The prophets in the form of God's pathos

The 'theomorphism', 'God-shapedness', of Israel's understanding of man is most clearly expressed in the prophets. It is a modern Jewish philosopher, Abraham Heschel, who has drawn attention to the inadequacy of treating the prophetic witness in terms of the 'word' alone. The prophetic word, oracle, teaching, hé insists, is always a word filled with the 'pathos' of the prophet's life. Heschel sets out to combat a view of classical Israelite prophecy which would disregard the prophet's part in the prophetic act by insisting on the absolutely objective and supernatural nature of prophecy. But equally, he is tilting against the kind of psychological imperialism which would deduce prophecy entirely from the inner life of the prophet, disregarding his awareness of a confrontation with a reality underived from himself. These are two opposing errors which tend to throw up each other by way of reaction. Surely we should begin rather from the prophet's life in the form into which it was moulded by God's hand. The perceptual pattern of prophetic vision is dependent, importantly, on this existential pattern of the prophet's life. His vision is a sharing of God's perspective on the world, seen in and from the perspective of the prophet's own situation. It is an 'exegesis of existence from a divine perspective'.[33]

The fundamental experience of the prophet, as Heschel so splendidly evokes that in his essay The Prophets, is one of fellowship with the feelings of God. It is a communion with the divine consciousness, brought about by the prophet's personal sharing in the divine pathos. Whether that affective concern of God for his people Israel be manifested as love or mercy, disappointment or anger, such feeling conveys the 'profound intensity of the divine inwardness'. By sympathy, literally a 'solidarity in pathos', the prophet's emotional life becomes assimilated to the divine. In his own being he finds the concrete embodiment of God's relation to Israel. He is a man who does not merely live out his own personal life but God's life too. The sensibility which characterizes this prophetic sympathy enables the prophet to hear God's voice and to feel his heart.

> The divine pathos is like a bridge over the abyss that separates man from God. It implies that the relationship between God and man is not dialectic, characterised by opposition and tension. Man in his essence is not the antithesis of the divine, although in his actual existence he may be rebellious and defiant. The fact that the attitudes of man may affect the life of God, that God stands in an intimate relationship to the world, implies a certain analogy between Creator and creature. The prophets stress not only the discrepancy of God and man, but also the relationship of reciprocity, consisting of God's engagement to man, not only of man's commitment to God. The disparity between God and the world is overcome in God, not in man.[34]

Heschel introduces the term 'theomorphic anthropology' in connection with that central command of the Holiness Code which is such a vital text for the Priestly School:

> Ye shall be holy, for I the Lord your God am holy!'

The prophetic passion is theomorphic because it expresses a call to an existence which will reproduce the pathos of God towards man. The prophet shares in God's holiness by standing in a relation to Israel isomorphic with God's own. This process begins when the divine pathos overwhelms the inner life of the prophet, taking possession of his heart and mind. Yet nothing could be more alien to the prophets than the inculcation of a life of religious feeling for its own sake, a kind of Yahwistic *éducation sentimentale*. The prophet has a ministry to perform. His life has to give public and visible form to his feeling so that he may be a sign for the presence and demands of God in Israel's history. Prophetic sympathy generates a tension between the sense of what is and the sense of what ought to be. It finds its resolution and its goal in public events, in the transformation of Israel as she stands before the living God. Prophetic existence, then, takes place *in foro publico*. Indeed, not only is it lived out in the public *forum*, it has of its essence a public *form*, a visible shape and pattern which is focused in the 'signs' which the great prophets acted out as ritualized expressions of the meaning of their life and ministry. So it was, for instance, that Isaiah's 'sign' in wandering through the streets of Jerusalem naked and barefoot symbolized the divine pathos he preached, God's dereliction at the pride and folly of Judah.[35] Other examples are scattered through the scrolls of Jeremiah and Ezekiel.[36] These moments of enacted parable take their force from the extended enacted parable which is the prophet's life. The form of that life bodies forth a pathos of infinitely loving and ethically and religiously demanding concern in which human feelings and interests are drawn up out of their finitude. But, so Heschel contends, such absolute selflessness and mysteriously undeserved love as we find in the pattern of the prophet's life are more akin to the divine than to the human. If these characteristics are really ascribed to the Hebrew prophets then the Old Testament is witnessing that these men were graciously endowed by God with the attributes of the divine.

If we put together the theomorphic picture of man in the Hebrew Bible and its anthropomorphic language about God we find ourselves placed in the presence of 'the signs for a God who is not alien to the human but makes himself a sharer in a human way in the history of man'.[37] The heritage of anthropomorphic discourse about God in Israel is not, as hellenized Jews like Philo seem to have thought, a merely uncriticized and residual piece of archaic belief. It holds a quite conscious theological affirmation, the confession of the God-who-is-present-in-the-form-of-the-human.[38]

Let us look a little more closely at two such human 'images' that carry a divine disclosure, the prophet Hosea and the prophet Jeremiah. Hosea's 'revelation' is made in and through a human experience in which, as Wheeler Robinson finely wrote, 'the truth to be revealed is first created'.[39] His teaching stems from the form of his

27

relationship with Gomer his wife. She married Hosea despite a past history of promiscuity and repaid him by going in for cultic prostitution at the shrines of Ba'al. His fidelity to her despite her unfaithfulness to him proves the pattern in which, as Hosea saw it, his whole existence was moulded. In this form he perceives a disclosure of Yahweh's purposes for Israel, and thereby he finds God revealed as the God of grace. Just as Hosea's continued love for Gomer goes beyond all merely sensible human calculation, passing beyond the pale of Israel's criminal law which decreed a very different fate for an adulteress, so God's love for the harlot Israel belongs to the secret of his inner being, closed off to man's probing.

> I will betroth you to myself for ever, betroth you with integrity and justice, with tenderness and love; I will betroth you to myself with faithfulness, and you will come to know Yahweh.[40]

Hosea's teaching is not some allegorical pirouette danced on the stage of his life-story. Rather, he discerns in the form of his life, in the meaningful pattern it has acquired out of the most unlikely materials, from turbulent events and even more turbulent emotions, the very expression of God's own pathos towards his people. He sees in the form of his life the sacrament or image of that pathos, its visible revelation.

Jeremiah's case is, if anything, more remarkable still. Here the relation between God's pathos and the form of prophetic existence has left a more direct literary precipitate in the shape of fragments of autobiographical poetry, scattered through the book of Jeremiah. Jeremiah felt himself to have been a 'thought of God'[41] before the divine hands moulded his limbs to the pattern of that thought. This divine moulding entailed the whole destiny with which he struggled so humanly and poignantly. He was made to be, in his own words, a visible 'fortified city' in the sight of all the nation.[42] Agonized by an intense spiritual conflict, pleading for Israel yet accusing her too in her guilt, he found himself expressing to his contemporaries the divine pathos towards them. Possibly the image of his life influenced the delineation of the figure of the Suffering Servant in the Isaianic corpus and thereby profoundly affected the Jewish picture of the expected divine mediator, 'he who cometh'.[43] Jeremiah expressed unforgettably the tension between the will to confer salvation and

28

the will to require justice in God himself. In all this Jeremiah is 'the human image of God who suffers over Israel, because he loves her and thus must judge her'.[44]

This aspect of revelation is not limited to the prophetic books. There are analogies to the figures we have glanced at in the presentation of Moses in the Pentateuch and in the figure of the Davidic king in the Psalter. But the central point seems established. Through a process of interpretation of experience Hosea and Jeremiah emerge as living 'images' of God. It is the form of their lives which discloses the God they speak of and for in their oracles, To see how they communicate knowledge of the character of God we find ourselves invoking the idea of the artwork, of the selection and composition of materials which shows us a striking shape standing out against its background, a 'significant form'. They disclose God as the artist of their lives. We are reminded how a great philosophical exponent of prophetic faith, Sören Kierkegaard, once expressed the hope that he might 'gesture' with his whole subjectivity. In 'The Difference between a Genius and an Apostle' he says that if a man were able to become an apostle in such a way that the whole depth of his subjectivity were transformed into a function of the One who sent him, then it might be possible for him to make the paradox of faith credible in a genuinely Christian way, the paradox that God is, for Christian faith, a particular man, *this* particular man lost in history.[45]

CHAPTER THREE

Christ the Image of God

We have seen so far that the potential significance of the cult image for evoking the divine is transferred in the Priestly theology of the Hebrew Bible to man himself. It is man who is the locus of God's self-disclosure. The aniconic quality of classical Yahwistic faith leaves the way open for the recognition of the significant form in human lives which can 'portray' the divine pathos in Israel. We must turn now to the New Testament affirmation that in Jesus Christ the divine has been embodied in an ultimately satisfying image, placing that affirmation in the context of the thought and aspirations of the world in which it came to expression.

The voices of later Judaism

We shall consider here the evidence for the role of the theme of the image in Jewish teaching and Jewish hopes for the future after the close of the Old Testament period. Inter-testamental Judaism and the rabbinic Judaism whose written monuments follow after the New Testament have great continuities as well as discontinuities, and it is generally recognized that much of the rabbinic material must apply to the common teaching of the first century A.D., even though we are not able to date it with any precision unless it is attached to more celebrated rabbis. There is something to be said, therefore, for listening to the 'voices of later Judaism' together; that should give us the resonance of the Jewish world in which Paul, the first Christian theologian of Christ the Image, was active.[1]

Basically, Jewish thought at this time preserved the theological anthropology of the Priestly Document, bud modified that teaching in two directions. Most important, the concern with man's final and God-given destiny which derived from the Apocalyptists gave people a strong incentive to search the accounts of the Beginning for ways of speaking about the fulfilment of God's creative and redemptive plan at the End. In a very different vein, a more speculative interest in natural theology arising in Hellenistic Jewish Wisdom from the naive natural theology of the older sapiential materials also utilized the metaphor of the image to speak of God's presence in the world.

The idea of a total destruction of the divine image with the Fall is nowhere unambiguously present.[2] It was not, in Jewish tradition, a natural reading of the Pentateuch. What the rabbis do describe, however, is a diminishing, darkening, and suspending of man's capacity to image God, whenever actual sin takes hold of his life – which is very often indeed. In quarters where no lively expectations of a fresh divine self-disclosure in man's world were entertained there was, perhaps, a tendency to reduce the significance of man's imaging of God to purely ethical terms. The metaphor is in some danger of becoming a mere rubric for 'the dignity of man', 'Whoever despises a man', says a logion ascribed to Rabbi Tanchuma, 'should realize that this one whom he despises God made in his image.'[3] Jakob Jervell in his survey of the extant literature on the 'image of God' in late Judaism interpreted the rather fragmentary evidence to mean that in the mainstream of rabbinic thought the image had indeed been imperilled or even temporarily lost by Adam but was restored at least as a possibility, by the gift of the Torah at Sinai.[4] More recent scholarship suggests that the function of the Sinai and Torah theologies in the traditions he discusses is rather to explain how man must live now if God is to grant him *in the future* eternal life and with that the full radiance of the divine image.[5] The new nature, redeeming men from the evil of the present Age, always remains a gift of the Age to come, despite its dependence for any given individual on a life of obedience to the Torah. Since the motif of the image and the motif of Adam are in Jewish exegesis most closely interrelated we are justified in saying that it was common teaching in the world where the New Testament came to birth that through the Law the Jew could not stand in the condition of man in the divine image in the full sense envisaged by rabbis and apocalyptists alike, but he could prepare himself to receive that image in the new world to be brought in by God.

As a student of the background of Paul's doctrine of Christ as

31

the last Adam has brought out, the theme of the image and the theme of Adam feed each other subterraneously without being brought together into a well-defined theological structure.[6] Yet the connection is vital since Adam's nature becomes for many writers in the period a description of God's intent for man, an intention 'realised once in the person of Adam, to be consummated by all believers in the age to come.'[7] There is a hope, that is, for a God-given fulfilment of the partial and fitful disclosure of the divine in humanity, by the raising up of a new Adam who will be God's perfected image. One passage, however, gives us the link we need. A haggadic tale about the Tannaitic Rabbi Bana'ah tells of the divine voice which deterred him from visiting the tomb of Adam among the patriarchal graves: 'You have seen the image of my likeness, but you may not see my likeness itself'. The passage teaches that Adam is God's primordial image, his beauty passed down to worthy Israelites and reflected in the faces of various celebrated rabbis. Through the Shekinah, the presence of the divine Glory, his being is the reflecting image of God.[8] The extraordinary exaltation the figure of Adam undergoes in texts like this springs from a retrojection of the hope for God's New Man: if the new nature of humanity in the Age to Come is to be equated with God's original intent for man, then Adam must have existed in the condition the blessed will share some day in the future. In the *Apocalypse of Moses* Adamic man recovers his glory at the turn of the Ages, and is set as God's vice-gerent 'on the throne of thy deceiver'.[9] Humanity is remade in the divine likeness, and reigns radiant with the splendour of God's self-disclosure.

In the later Wisdom literature we seem to move in a different ambience altogether. According to the Book of Wisdom, wisdom is 'an effulgence from everlasting light, and an unspotted mirror of the working of God, and an image of his goodness.'[10] This 'wisdom' is God's bestowal of a capacity on creation which enables it to grant an order to men's lives.[11] The primeval world order, the mystery behind the creation of the world to which man and nature alike must conform, reflects God's own light, activity, and goodness. No human life can be 'in the image' unless it responds to this cosmic image of God. The Wisdom of Solomon connects its teaching with the aniconicism of Israel, arguing that the making of images is folly since God the Creator can be recognized in what he himself has proposed as his 'image': creation. This is a true natural theology which differs widely in shape from what was elsewhere understood as revelation in Israel. Yet it is not impossible to throw across some nets to draw the 'image' in creation and the 'image' in the form of life of the servants of Yahweh together. We shall see how just that was done in the light of the coming of Christ by the Letter to the Colossians. Any figure that does 'image' God must, by the yardstick of Wisdom, also provide the key to a sense of God's cosmic purposes in creating.

The art of the synagogue

It is not too much to say, in view of the kind of expectations for a disclosure of God's Glory in the new Adam that we have described, and, the subject of this next section, the utterly unexpected rise of a theological art in the Jewish synagogue in our period, that we are dealing here with a quite special historical moment in the life of the Jewish people. It is an epoch in which the divine is being looked for on the faces of men. To some extent this is the result of the Jewish community's being touched by a widespread sensibility of the late antique world. Peter Brown has written that 'throughout the Mediterranean world, face and halo tend to come together in late antiquity'.[12] But to a perhaps greater extent it is the renaissance of a specifically Old Testament idea of revelation.

Paul's time was a period in which a rich visual art was being born in the heart of the synagogue. In the synagogue mosaics of Ain-ed-Duk and Beth Alpha and the sculptings in the Galilean synagogues,[13] at the Villa Torlonia in Rome[14], and above all at Dura-Europos,[15] we have evidence of a burgeoning art in both two and three dimensional forms, a great part of which is being put to theological service. At Beth-Alpha, daringly enough, we find a depiction of the hand of God in the scene of Isaac's sacrifice. At Dura-Europos, in early third-century murals which replaced an earlier scheme (now unfortunately irrecoverable) in the first-century synagogue, we can see the divine hand lifting up Ezekiel by his hair. And in the iconographic scheme at Dura as a whole the entire divine action in history by which the God of Israel was named and

33

blessed in the Jewish Liturgy is disclosed to the worshipper in the sequences of narrative art.

We should linger a moment over Dura, for it is by far the most complete artistic witness to Jewish religious sensibility in the period of the birth of Christianity that we have. Let us cast our eye around the synagogue room. We see a box relieved only by the Torah shrine on one wall – until, that is, we have taken in the shapes that beckon to us from the murals. The panel above the Torah shrine is a kind of open triptych with paintings of decisive moments in the life of Moses: Moses and the burning bush, Moses on Mount Sinai, Moses reading the scroll of the Torah, Moses after his death surrounded by sun, moon, and stars. Elsewhere we have a fragment of Jacob's dream. On the back wall Moses leads out the people from Egyptian bondage; Joshua encompasses Jericho bearing the Ark; the Israelites fight the Philistine host at Ebenezer; the Ark leaves Ekron of Philistia. The synagogue also boasts a sequence which seems to blend a haggadic tale about the fountain of Miriam and the biblical accounts of Moses' water miracles. In the lowest zone of the north wall come illustrations of the visions of Ezekiel, the main motif being the resurrection of Israel. There is an Elijah sequence leading up to the raising of the son of the widow of Zarephath; a scene for the anointing of David and one of Ahasuerus on Solomon's throne between Esther and Mordecai. Only God's hand appears in the paintings but this is enough to indicate how this iconography should be read. It is the visual evocation of God's will in act among his people. At the same time, the style of the paintings shows a fascination with the portrayal of faces. The emphasis on the eyes, which have an animation rare in antique statuary or painting, communicates a sense of profound religious interiority. This is especially notable in the figure of Ezekiel (despite its poor technical execution) and in the splendid figure of the young prophet holding the Torah. The faithful at Dura were engaged in the history of God's showing of himself in history through an interplay with the light shining in the faces of the saints of Israel.

At a catacomb in Beth Shearim we can see the figure of a man standing with the menorah, the 'candlestick all of gold, with a bowl upon the top of it, and its seven lamps thereon' which represents the divine dwelling in Israel in the oracles of Zechariah.[16] In the exegesis of the time, the menorah is taken as a symbol of Israel and

34

the bowl which surmounts it (possibly a receptacle for water, to extinguish the pieces of falling wick) as a symbol for God. It is well within the limits of the evidence for Jewish symbols in the early Christian period, concludes a major scholar of the subject, to see in the belief that the just were to become like the menorah 'a particular example of the belief that they were to become like God. Beholding his glory, as one Jew said, they were to be "changed into that same image, from glory to glory"'.[17] Now it is the case that the material best dated to the first century in Palestine has very little in the way of human figures. This may possibly imply that a more rigorous pharisaic-rabbinic Judaism removed a certain amount of iconography in the period between the fall of the Temple and the disastrous Bar Cochba revolt, the period when the Pharisaic authorities were in command of the nation's religious life. It is surely quite impossible to suppose with Goodenough that more rigorous Pharisees were able to enforce a total ban on images in the entire epoch from the Maccabees to A.D. 70. They were effectively in power only for intervals; far less than would be needed for control of the decorative art of the entire country. It may be that a conflict over the rise of this art has left its detritus in the later rabbinic viewpoint that the making of figures of any kind for any purpose is forbidden. This was no part of the original Torah: it represents part of the 'hedge' the rabbis put up to protect the Law from encroachment by demanding more than it did itself.[18] Perhaps it was the evidence for a new Jewish interest in art-images that led them to plant their hedge around the aniconic commandments. Be that as it may, the ground must have been under preparation, as Morton Smith says, in the first century for the fantastic explosion of human and divine symbols in the second and third.[19] It does not seem excessive to claim that the emergence of an art of the kind we have traced lies somewhere in the penumbra of connotation of the Pauline language of the 'image of God'.

The realization of the image: the Christian Lord in Pauline perspective

In an assembly of the Christian church at Colossae, a city of the Lycus valley about a hundred miles east of the Asia Minor coast at Ephesus, the first Christian generation celebrated in a brief, exultant

35

hymn the embodied fulfilment of the old revelation to Israel in the person of a crucified Jewish teacher, Jesus of Nazareth. The hymn, which may be found in the Letter to the Colossians 1. 15–20, is about creation and redemption, and sees Jesus as the key to both. It proclaims him, in fact the 'image of the invisible God'. Possibly the Colossian Christians had been given the hymn by Paul himself on the journey mentioned in the Acts of the Apostles.[20] Possibly it broke on them fresh with the Letter itself. Possibly it was the composition of another hymnwriter soaked in Pauline thought and so was eminently apt for Paul's purposes in writing to Colossae.

In the Lycus valley the Christian faith appears to have been spiced in the early days with the flavour of that Jewish speculation about God's revelation in the historical and cosmic process, as we have described that in the preceding lines of this chapter. To Paul's eyes the images of God appealed to in Jewish wisdom and apocalyptic writing were not so much false as outclassed.[21] To fail to recognize that in Jesus Christ God had been disclosed in an image that was unique, definitive, and devastating in its overwhelmingness was at best pitiable, at worst infidelity to the perceived truth. The nub of Paul's contrast between the Christian vision and the opacity of the brethren at Colossae lies in his awareness of Jesus as the wholly adequate image of God's being whereas the angels, the presiding spirits of the cosmos venerated at Colossae, were only a hierarchy of limited communication and revelation between God and man. Paul supposes, along with many contemporary Jews, that the angels mediated the gift of the Mosaic Law.[22] In the days before his Damascus road vision of the exalted Christ he would, no doubt, have shared the common rabbinic view that the Torah is a partial, but only partial remedy for Adam's loss of the active power to be God's self-disclosure in the world. As a convert to the new faith he had given classical expression to the deficiencies of the Law in any making good of what was lost with Adam in his Letter to the Romans. Paul showed there that to attempt to use the Mosaic Torah as a way of salvation was to misapply it. Trying to bridge the gulf between God and man from God's side through the Law is beating the air, for the whole point of the Law is to reveal the need for a new, creative act of God towards man. This act took place in Christ, so that mankind can live from then on by the 'law' (that is, the way of life, the personal and corporate regime) of 'the

36

Spirit of life in Christ Jesus.[23] Similarly, here at Colossae where he is faced with a rather different face of the polymorphous Judaism of his day, Paul concludes that if God's perfect embodiment in the human has appeared in a uniquely privileged image, Jesus Christ, then the whole era of relating to God *via* the Torah is over and done with. The cosmic disclosures of God which the Colossians associate with the Law's angelic mediators must be subordinate now to the disclosure in Jesus. They are hopelessly inadequate and unsatisfying in comparison.

The text of the Hymn may be set out in a way that suggests its formal structure, the much-favoured one known as 'chiasm' where words and ideas are repeated in reverse order to produce a powerful cumulative effect:

> a He is the image of the invisible God
> b The first-born of all creation;
> c For in him all things were created,
> α in heaven
> β and on earth
> β visible
> α and invisible
> α' whether thrones (visible)
> β' or dominions (invisible)
> β' or principalities (invisible)
> α' or powers (visible)
> a All things were created through him and for him:
> he is before all things
> And in him all things hold together.
> He is the head of the body (the church).
> α' He is the beginning,
> β' The first-born from the dead (that in everything he might be pre-eminent)
> β' For in him all the fulness of God was pleased to dwell,
> α' And through him to reconcile to himself all things,
> Making peace by the blood of his cross,
> Whether on earth,
> Or in heaven.[24]

So Christ, according to this *credo* in hymn form, is the amply sufficient disclosure of God, rendering all others surpassed and jejune. Paul's conviction of the completeness of revelation and salvation in Christ is developed theologically to the point where he is identified with God's Word and God's Wisdom, the agents of his self-disclosure 'from the beginning'. The Aramaist C. F. Burney showed how the hymn achieves this by giving a motif from Jewish wisdom the key position in its structure.[25] Wisdom teachers had established a tradition of interpreting the opening words of Genesis which is exemplified in this passage and later influenced both the Rabbis and the Christian Fathers. Weighing the text of Genesis word by word, they found a clue to the meaning of its first words, 'in the beginning', in a second text concerned with creation, Proverbs 8.22. In the Greek version of this sapiential text in the Septuagint Bible it read

> The Lord created me (that is, Wisdom)
> as the beginning of his way.

The cross-reference, supposing that the Bible has an inner unity of meaning, enabled the Wisdom School to identify 'Wisdom' with 'the beginning' and so to take the opening noun construction of Genesis in an instrumental sense. They would then have

> Through the Beginning, that is, Wisdom,
> God created. . . .

The hymn-writer of Colossians, alive to these implications as only a deeply theologically read Jew would be, offers his readers an exposition of *Bereshith*, In the Beginning, in Christian terms. It pivots on the multiple senses that the preposition *be* and the noun *reshith* can bear:

Bereshith: in *reshith*	in him all things were created (1.15)
by *reshith*	all things were created through him (1.16)
into *reshith*	all things were created for him (1.16)

38

Reshith:	Beginning	he is before all things (1.17)
	Sum-total	in him all things hold together (1.17)
	Head	he is the head of the body (1.18)
	First-fruits	he is the beginning, the first-born from the dead (1.18)

As Burney writes,

> The conclusion is that, in every possible sense of the expression, Christ is its fulfiller.[26]

Hence he may be said to hold the key to that revelation of God in his world which lies as the mystery at the heart of Jewish Wisdom. By looking on this image, we discover the authoritative interpretation of cosmos and history. Jesus re-interprets in a decisive fashion the whole realm of the real. The claim is breathtaking. The reader may wonder whether an ancient writer, who left no ordered speculative system, no *Summa Theologiae* or *Phänomenologie des Geistes,* can really have intended to be taken in this sense. Paul's methods are the tortuous or mannered ones of rabbinic exegetical techniques and the diatribe of the Hellenistic market-place, but his goals are universal. C. K. Barrett has well said that:

> Paul was not a systematic theologian but he laid the foundations for systematic theology, partly by the unwearying mental vitality with which he worked at every problem he encountered in the course of his Christian activity and thinking, and partly through a natural capacity not merely for seeing both sides of a question but for holding them together, and at such a temperature that they became fused into a unitary scheme of thought. As such a theologian, he conceives a picture of God's dealings with humanity as a whole. These form a single story with an intelligible meaning, for it is the work of one person, God, who acts throughout with a consistent (though often mysterious) purpose. Paul's conception of this story and this purpose is sometimes described as a philosophy of history. There is truth in this description, for Paul does (though unsystematically) attempt to show the coherence of the theological process. The description is, however,

39

inadequate for it is not a rational coherence that Paul finds in history, but a personal and theological coherence.[27]

But how did Paul come to ascribe this role of conferring coherence on history to Jesus? And how did he arrive at the idea of decanting this universal significance of Jesus by a theology of the image?

To answer these questions we must turn to his earlier correspondence with the church in Corinth where the theology that comes to serene and monumental expression in the Colossians hymn may be glimpsed being hammered out in polemic. Paul's Corinthian letters, like all his writing, presuppose a reading of the significance of Jesus' person and ministry at a deeper level than that represented by such meagre factual allusions to Jesus' life and teaching as can be picked out from that writing. To concentrate purely on these is to neglect an essential of all historical interpretation. The significance of any historical figure would remain shrouded if the sequel to his life and death were excluded from the reckoning.[28] If Paul's claim to 'have the mind of Christ'[29] is well-founded it will be because of a certain distance whereby he could stand back and see the meaning of the words and actions of Jesus – including the immensely mysterious ones involved in the Resurrection appearances, – taking on a particular configuration, crystallizing into a significant form. Quite naturally in these matters of hermeneutics we find ourselves using the language of aesthetic perception which Paul himself adopts in giving his teaching on Jesus the Christ to the Corinthian church.[30]

A text without a context is a pretext. Günther Bornkamm wrote:

> The distinctiveness of the Pauline letters lies in their being close to the living voice of the gospel, that is to say, the gospel proclaimed by word of mouth and aimed at gaining both a hearing and an obedience in faith. They do not move in the realm of abstract theoretical reflection, but always include the hearers' own situation as a determining factor. . . . (In addition) Paul's letters differ from countless other church treatises and pastoral epistles both early and late in that their author's person and work are an indissoluble unity. The modern reader will often feel their strangeness, nor should he try to gloss over it. But he should also be conscious that here the power of the spirit is united with the power of the heart and finds expression in language which

is often quite amazing in its mastery. Very often it is difficult, impenetrable and overloaded; it shifts and changes, being wooing, and gracious, but abrupt and harsh as well. In every case, however, it is dictated by the apostle's work and gospel. It is a tool used by a man who is himself a tool in the hand of his master.[31]

The difficulties Paul encountered at Corinth, that problem child among his churches, were twofold. First, there were people at Corinth convinced that their claims to mystical and charismatic experience allowed them to dismiss Paul's teaching office as an apostle in favour of their own individual wisdom. Second, substantial disagreements existed there over the substance of the Christian gospel itself, as distinct from its mode of transmission. It was over these doctrinal headings, apparently, that a Corinthian delegation reached Paul at his missionary base of Ephesus in the spring of 54 or 55, and their report evoked his reply in the form of 1 Corinthians (actually his second letter to that church). Identical or very similar misunderstandings about the relation of personal experience to Paul's office in the structure of the community of Jesus persisted, however. Soon they were exacerbated by the arrival of Jewish-Christian missionaries hostile to Paul. These men either directly fostered them, or at least used them to lever Paul from his position of influence in his daughter-church. Finally, this crisis provoked, a year or more later, the dispatch from Macedonia of 2 Corinthians which includes a striking discussion of the relationship of Christ, the Christian apostle and the Christian, expressed through the metaphor of the image. In 1 Corinthians exploring the meaning of the resurrection of Jesus leads Paul to invoke the metaphor. In 2 Corinthians it is introduced to serve his affirmation that the apostle despite, or because of, his human weakness has a divine part to play on earth. The theme amounts to a demonstration, evidently, of the truth of Bornkamm's judgment of the Letters.

Our survey of the late Jewish sources should prepare us for the discovery that in 1 Corinthians the metaphor of the image is inextricably involved with Paul's teaching on the first and last Adam.

If there is a physical body, there is also a spiritual body. Thus it is written, 'The first man Adam became a living being'; the

41

last Adam became a life-giving spirit. But it is not the spiritual which is first but the physical, and then the spiritual. The first man was from the earth, a man of dust; the second man is from heaven. As was the man of dust, so are those who are of the dust; and as is the man of heaven, so are those who are of heaven. Just as we have borne the image of the man of dust, we shall also bear the image of the man of heaven.[32]

In this passage Paul is not trying to show that the general notion of resurrection from the dead is a valid one. For him, as for all Pharisaic Jews, that general notion was unproblematic, for the concept of God's faithfulness to Israel was held to entail another world of ethical justice to set against the world in which the wicked prosper. He aims to give 'assurance to the Christian just what kind of existence is to be his and how it is to be obtained.'[33] Not Adam, the father of empirical humanity, but Jesus, the Christ or 'Spirit-anointed' head of a new humanity, discloses to man the hope of a transfigured humanity which God wills for him. To convey his teaching Paul takes over a slightly abstruse exegetical pattern. In Genesis 2.7 we hear of how God breathed his own spirit into Adam's form so that he became a living body. A rabbinic text, taking its cue from the doubling of the letter *yod* in the Yahwist's verb *wayyit-ser*, 'he formed', offered a midrashic expansion of the scripture to expound the Jewish doctrine of resurrection.[34] The word, it was said, denotes two formations. One is man's nature in this world, the other his nature of the world to come. (Of course this is scarcely convincing exegesis, but it served well enough for the theological communication the rabbis were making.) Paul makes the *midrash* his own. 'The first Adam became a living soul, the last Adam (that is, Jesus) became a life-giving Spirit.' In his body of glory Christ lives radiantly as true humanity, the realization at last of the possibility the writers of Genesis had seen in the human animal 'in the beginning'. In the glorious humanity of the risen Christ the expected humanity of the last Adam has been seen by men. Once he had glimpsed Christ, Paul had no doubt that he had located the model and means of transfiguring the form of human life into that condition where it is capable of imaging God, just as the Jewish apocalyptists had hoped man would 'in the last days'.

Paul had come to see Jesus, therefore, as a man who fulfilled the

42

spoilt promise of Adam and thus renewed the image of God in the human. The very lapse of time which distanced Paul from the historical Jesus enabled him to perceive what the artist Degas would call the 'essential gestures' of his life.[35] These essential gestures, in which the revelatory form of Jesus' life consists, are above all a matter of his perfect, creative obedience to God. That responsiveness in obedience to the Father, in life and in death, is for Paul the inverted image of Adam's sin. Christ, although he was in the form (or image) of God, did not exploit the existence with God which he possessed, but renounced his claims, choosing instead the way of humiliation and obedience manifested in the carpenter's home at Nazareth and the *via dolorosa* to Calvary.

> His state was divine,
> yet he did not cling
> to his equality with God
> but emptied himself
> to assume the condition of a slave,
> and became as men are;
> and being as all men are,
> he was humbler yet,
> even to accepting death,
> death on a cross.
> But God raised him high
> and gave him the name
> which is above all other names
> so that all beings
> in the heavens, on earth and in the underworld
> should bend the knee at the name of Jesus
> and that every tongue should acclaim
> Jesus Christ as Lord,
> to the glory of God the Father.[36]

In this canticle of praise to Christ who is in the form, *morphe*, of God (v.6), the Paul of the Letter to the Philippians portrays Christ's exaltation against the foil of Adam's fate. Christ did not snatch at his destiny as Adam had tried to procure godhead. Instead, he received it as God's gift after treading this path of service of God and of man. Paul had no need to pepper his writing with historical

43

allusions to the geography and chronology of Jesus' personal history, nor to reproduce his *ipsissima verba*.[37] It was enough to have grasped the human form of Jesus' life as the embodiment of a transcendent self-giving and faithfulness recognized as the hallmarks of the divine from the Old Testament experience of Israel. It was enough to make out the contours of the existence of Jesus for this is, in itself, the disclosure of the Father. In a later and specifically Christological chapter we shall consider how the move from the perception of Jesus the revealer to the perception of Jesus the Son of God is achieved.[38] For the moment we shall stay with Paul, to complete our exploration of the rich veins of his teaching on the image of God in the letters to Corinth.

The expression of the image: the Christian disciple in the Corinthian mirror

In 2 Corinthians Paul moves on to further implications.[39] Since Jesus' life and death were 'for us', the effects of his person and work will hardly be sealed away in *apartheid* from the rest of the history of mankind. In dependence on the disclosure of God's glory in Christ revelation continues to be mediated *in the Church*, even in the absence of the visible Christ. The life of faith establishes a communion with Christ in which disciples are themselves transformed and become God's images by his grace. Barrett traces the structure of Paul's thought by pointing out that

> For Paul, 'Man' is a historical and individual term, for Jesus of Nazareth, who lived in ·Palestine in the first half of the first century and was crucified under Pontius Pilate, was the Man to come. But the same word is also an eschatological and collective term, for it denotes the new humanity that is to be in Christ, and is already partially and inadequately adumbrated in Christians. The full conception of the Man to come can be disclosed only at the last day, when the heavenly Man appears with the holy ones who are conformed to his image.[40]

Paul has been making a Christian commentary, in midrashic style, on a section of the book of Exodus. Since this is so Hebraic a piece of writing it has been suggested that it may have started life as a homily given by Paul to a Jewish audience in the synagogue. Exodus 34. 39–34 which he takes as his departure point, is the Priestly source's account of how Moses came down from Sinai after his meeting with Yahweh. He carried the tablets of the Torah, and his features were transfigured by the glory of God. Paul's aim is to bring out the splendour of the calling of an apostle in the new covenant dispensation which supersedes that of Moses. A veil had covered Moses' face because its radiance was painful to onlookers. Paul sees in this veil a symbol of the transitory and partial character of the old economy of divine revelation. Moses' features had been briefly brilliant with the divine glory, no more, and their radiance dimmed when his single encounter with God was over. Since the veil can represent the incapacity of the Mosaic dispensation to show God fully to man, then, it may be said to be spread still over the minds of the Jews devoted as they are to the scrolls of the Torah rather than to the figure of Jesus. It will not be removed, indeed, until they turn to 'the Lord, who is the Spirit'.

Since we have such a hope, we are very bold, not like Moses who put a veil over his face so that the Israelites might not see the end of the fading splendour. But their minds were hardened; for to this day, when they read the old covenant, that same veil remains unlifted, because only through Christ is it taken away. Yes, to this day whenever Moses is read a veil lies over their minds; but when a man turns to the Lord the veil is removed. Now the Lord is the Spirit, and where the Spirit of the Lord is, there is freedom. And we all, with unveiled face, beholding the glory of the Lord, are being changed into his likeness [image] from one degree of glory to another; for this comes from the Lord who is the Spirit.[41]

This Lord (*Kurios*) who is the Spirit (*Pneuma*) enables disciples to go 'from glory to glory' until they are transformed into the image they contemplate. In contexts where he is engaged in a *re-lecture* of the Old Testament, as here, *ho Kurios* is for Paul not the Jesus who is Christ but the Yahweh of Israel himself.[42] He makes a kind of functional identification between the God of Israel to whom Moses turned on Sinai and found himself temporarily transfigured,

45

and the Holy Spirit of the new covenant. That is, he suggests that the kind of thing that the Lord of Israel was said to do in the Hebrew Bible the Spirit of Christ may equally legitimately be said to do in this new era of grace. Under this new covenant Moses' privilege of uncovering his face before the Lord's glory is made universal by the activity of the Holy Spirit. All Christian believers are, *eo ipso*, contemplatives. They are *hoi katoptrizomenoi*, men who can 'see as in a mirror' the very glory of God. The translation is sometimes controverted, for the Greek word could mean a passive reflecting rather than an active looking. In 1 Corinthians 13, 12, however, Paul states that there is indeed such a thing as Christian contemplation, even if complete mutuality of knowledge between God and man is reserved to the future. Aware, perhaps, that looking-glasses were made in Corinth he calls this contemplation 'looking through a glass and seeing obscurely'. To readers of *Alice through the Looking-Glass* the metaphor, and its preposition *dia*, 'through', will be easily understood. The virtual image produced by a plane mirror appears to lie on its further side. In Paul's use the glass is always an instrument of revelation, while his stress may lie sometimes on the indirectness of the seeing and sometimes on the seeing itself. The contemporary Greek-speaking Jew Philo had once prayed that he might 'see God's form in no other mirror than himself'.[43] For Paul this divine mirror is a concrete reality, the *face of Christ* whereby the 'light of the knowledge of God' is communicated to us. The face of Jesus is the crucial factor, therefore, in our own *transfiguration*.[44]

To identify the Pauline mirror we have anticipated slightly the movement of the argument in the Epistle. Christ's face is not mentioned explicitly until 4.4–6, a passage which relates the theme of the image to the office of the apostle and in so doing returns us by a different route to the central christological concerns of Pauline theology. Attached to Christ by faith, Paul thinks, a man will contemplate him unceasingly and be transformed progressively by this contemplation, so that eventually he can bring others, as the apostle himself brings them, to the light of the gospel.

Therefore, having this ministry by the mercy of God, we do not lose heart. We have renounced disgraceful, underhanded ways; we refuse to practise cunning or to tamper with God's word, but by the open statement of the truth we would commend ourselves to every man's conscience in the sight of God. And even if our gospel is veiled, it is veiled only to those who are perishing. In their case the god of this world has blinded the minds of the unbelievers, to keep them from seeing the light of the gospel of the glory of Christ, who is the likeness [image] of God. For what we preach is not ourselves, but Jesus Christ as Lord, with ourselves as your servants for Jesus' sake. For it is the God who said, 'Let light shine out of darkness', who has shone in our hearts to give the light of the knowledge of the glory of God in the face of Christ.[45]

The apostle becomes a slave to his hearers by devoting his life to them and so becomes for them an image of the Jesus who spent himself in self-giving.

Paul is not without a *theologia gloriae*, and indeed has his own paradoxical kind of triumphalism.[46]

If the radiance of the image of God in Christ is not communicated to believers by means of the apostolic preaching this is not through some defect in God's grace. The form of the man who stoops to be the servant of all is *capax gloriae*: it can exhibit the divine glory to all. Continuing blindness to the universal significance of Jesus can only be explained by reference to some ·sheerly irrational principle of evil which distorts men's vision of the object before their eyes. Paul for his part was convinced that if he re-creates the essential gestures of the life of Jesus by delivering himself up to death, or the threat of death, for man's salvation and from God's love, then the 'life of Jesus' will be palpable in his own body.

As the manifest ringleader of the Christian movement, the apostle draws upon himself the heaviest experience of suffering; as the one in whom the Gospel is manifested he can say that the life of Jesus not only will be revealed in the resurrection at the last day but already begins to become visible in his mortal flesh.[47]

So we come back to the controlling nerve of Paul's teaching on the image. The divine image was manifested in Christ, as in dependence on that manifestation it appears in the Christian apostle as well, through a form of life which shows forth to the world an extremity of self-giving, out of love and unto death.[48]

For New Testament faith (it would not be difficult to show the same structure as Paul's in accounts of revelation through Christ in John[49] and Hebrews,[50] even though these writers do not use the key metaphor of the image which is required to bring out that structure) one human life has expressed itself in a form which is inexhaustibly significant for the disclosure of God. The term 'image of God' may be applied to this life in a quite unique and eminent way. But if the signs that make up the shape and contours of this life and the face which communicates its distinctive affective character as a life of utterly unbounded exemplification of 'grace and truth' disclose God's glory in unsurpassable fashion, then we may expect something to follow which did in fact follow in Christian history. The appearing of a supreme image throws open the way for the creation of a theological art apt to serve as exegesis of this new situation of the embodied disclosure of God in man. If God has elected to show himself definitively in the form of a human life, then may not the artist shape and fashion visual images which will add up to an exegesis of revelation? Christian art in the first centuries of the Church's life did quite naturally produce a world of meanings by its images in order to bring out a part, at least, of the meaning of the significant form of Christ. In so doing, artists threw light on the nature of revelation itself by offering us a model, the model of the artwork, in which to understand the revelatory disclosure.

CHAPTER FOUR

The Art of God in the World of the Fathers

I have suggested that, applying the model of the artwork to bring out the essentially aesthetic structure of revelation, the rise of a Christian art can be seen as the most natural consequence of the central Christian facts. Art should be able to offer an account of the meaning of a revelation that took place through a 'significant form'. Christianity would be untrue to itself if it could not so interpret itself and come thereby to a clearer grasp of its own revelational structure. Yet an enormous struggle over the making and veneration of images was necessary before these entailments could be clearly discerned. The impression has been given that the role of art in the early Church, that vital period in the formation of Christian theology and sensibility, was either insignificant or, worse, under the dark cloud of heterodoxy. In this chapter we shall be concerned to dispel this illusion, noting some of the connections of art, doctrine, and piety in the age of the Fathers, and assessing the strengths and weaknesses of such notions of aesthetics as may be found there. I begin, therefore, by looking at the evidence for the rise of Christian iconography, turning after that to glance at the flourishing life of the metaphor of the image in patristic christology and finish in the next chapter by considering the great struggle in which the conflicting traditions in art and christology found themselves engaged, the Iconoclast crisis.

The rise of Christian iconography

In the latter part of the last century a catena of literary citations about art in the early Church was under construction in Germany. The presuppositions scholars brought to interpreting the, admittedly fragmentary, evidence included most importantly a faulty

reading of the idea of spirit in the Fourth Gospel. Pietist Protestant-
ism and philosophical Idealism conspired to suggest that Christian
worship in the Gospel of John was not so much worship in the
(Holy) Spirit[1] as in the inner spirit of man. It was further assumed
that the Mosaic prohibition involved a total veto on images, scru-
pulously observed in Judaism and taken as equally authoritative by
the early Church.[2] We have seen that the Jewish part of this assumption is no more than a particular, rigorist rabbinic interpretation
and flies in the face of the synagogue art of the time. (Dura had not
been uncovered then.) As for the Christian Church's attitude to the
Decalogue it is impossible to draw any consistent teaching from the
comments of the Christian Fathers on the subject. Clement of Alexandria, at least, saw it symbolically,[3] and it was not until the
Valentinian heretic Ptolemy undertook the task in the mid-second
century that any real attempt was made to analyse the meaning of
the Old Testament Law for the life of the church.[4] Sister Charles
Murray of the Sisters of Notre Dame has shown[5] that we are dealing
here with a pervasive and canonized misunderstanding about the
whole business which should probably be traced back to Renan. In
his *Histoire des Origines du Christianisme* Renan made Christianity
a normatively iconophobic religion because of its Jewish matrix.[6]

Just at the time when the conviction was settling over German
universities that the rise of Christian art was no more than a movement of ill-evangelized and superstitious masses against the gospel
purity of church teachers the English divine B. F. Westcott was
producing a much more balanced estimate of the position.[7] True,
Westcott incorporated iconoclast interpretations of some early
Christian documents which may be dubious, but he made three
very valuable points against the religious despisers of artistic forms.
Firstly there was an *a priori* point: the centrality for Christian faith
of the embodiment of the divine in the human assumes a 'twofold
conception of the spiritual destiny of the visible, and of a spiritual
revelation through the visible'.[8] Working out the consequences and
entailments of that might be a slow business yet it is simply in the
nature of the Christian case that it must eventually construct a
theological aesthetic and find its own meaning in its artworks.

It is impossible that the facts of the Incarnation and Resurrection
can leave Art in the same position as before. The interpretation

50

of Nature and the embodiment of thought and feeling through outward things must assume a new character when it is known not only that Creation is the expression of the will of God and in its essence 'very good', but also that in humanity it has been taken into personal fellowship with the Word, through whom it was called into being.

Christian revelation, which discloses the pattern of existence through the light of the supreme interpretative image of Christ, has got to relate to art as 'a fresh birth, a transfiguration of all human powers, by the revelation of their divine connexions and destiny'.[9] Secondly, Westcott saw that the extremely early evidence of the art of the catacombs in the official burial-place of the Roman church must figure importantly in the case for the defence of the icons.[10] Thirdly, he pointed out, the liturgical and typological richness of the images in the catacombs seems to eliminate the notion that Christian iconography began with rude and imperfectly christian-ized masses – and he cautiously but clearly drew his readers' atten-tion to the theory of De Rossi that the first Christian artists worked under the direction of theologians and embodied definite schemes of doctrine in their pictures.[11] We may, however, recognize an element of truth in the Germanic picture of a lay movement working subterraneously – but not subversively – in the Church. For it is clear that a full-scale theology of images (as distinct from a theology in images or even the setting of theological programmes for images) came on the scene late in the day. Christian art began not as a speculation but as a thoroughly intelligible impulse of distinctively Christian faith, hope, and love among the people of God. The instinct which created it is not perhaps the poorest example of that *sensus fidelium* in which John Henry Newman liked to see the 'infallibility of the laity'.

The early Church created three types of artistic form to express her faith – or, rather, filled existing forms with a new content which gradually called forth its own proper stylistic expression. First of all, we find the simplest symbolic forms, associated chiefly with the catacombs of the Christian dead. So, for instance, we find the baptismal symbol of Christ the Fisher of men rescuing men with his rod from 'the buffeting seas of this world'.[12] The fish, the Greek word for which (ICHTHUS) formed an acrostic 'Jesus Christ Son of God Saviour' was a favoured motif, especially for the Eucharist. The shapes of a veiled, praying figure with raised hands, and of a dove bearing an olive branch in its beak symbolized the Christian in peace, *anima . . . in pace* as the inscriptions have it.

> Already, in the earliest frescoes of the Roman catacombs, shortly after 200, the sacramental sources of immortality, the fount of life and the food of life, are shown on the graves, and under the veil of those same symbols as were already used in the Gospels. Even Christ himself can only be seen in symbolic form: as the shepherd or the teacher.[13]

Then, more elaborately, on basilica walls we find the *historiae*, great sequences of narrative art of the kind we noted in the Jewish synagogue at Dura, the visual evocation of God's saving acts in history. As a foremost authority on early Christian church life, F. van der Meer, has shown, it was these *historiae* to which Christians would point in order to show that vast, historical backcloth of disclosure of God which Christ, the supreme image, interpreted, as the culminating artwork in a series interprets the perhaps ambiguous images that have gone before. Thus we encounter Adam and Eve, Noah's ark, Abel and Melchizedek, the sacrifice of Isaac, Moses striking water from the rock, Jonah and the great fish, Daniel in the lion's den, the three young men in the burning fiery furnace. When taxed with the novelty of Christianity by pagans, 'Christian apologists would answer: our history goes back to the beginning of creation: our Christ has cast his glowing shadow in a thousand archetypal forms.'[14] On the walls of the Basilica of Santa Maria Maggiore we can still see a series of mosaics placed there by pope Sixtus III to depict scenes from the books of Genesis, Exodus, and Joshua. They are splendid achievements of an impressionist art, with a sumptuous use of colour. But artistic technique subserves in them a visionary reading of history, for they are at the same time magnificently composed icons. Let Van der Meer describe one example of this basilican art for us:

> In the foreground on the left we see the 'Hospitality of Abraham', the visit of the three mysterious travellers to Abraham's tent at the Oak of Mamre. We see how the three heavenly messengers,

the bearers of the Great Promise, draw near; we see Sarah laughing in her tent, and how Abraham waits on the three guests at table. But when the early christians contemplated the mosaic they would think of how Abraham 'saw three, yet worshipped one', and they would recognise, in the appearance of the travellers at Mamre, an appearance of God in the Three-in-One. For this reason, the mosaic worker has surrounded the head of the middle one of the three unknown men with a wreath of ethereal fire – a *nubes divina* – a divine cloud'.[14]

Finally, and perhaps most important for our subject, were the portraits. These were the first images to receive direct and explicit veneration in Christian sanctuaries. Those at Sant' Apollinare Nuovo are typical: the scriptural authors holding their scrolls gaze directly at the worshipper, as do the men and women martyrs in the lower zone as they process towards Christ and his mother. The expression of the eyes in these early portraits is as remarkable as it was at Dura: and it is this expressiveness which makes possible the personal encounter between the holy figure and the worshipper. Much further east, at Bawit in Egypt, a Coptic icon shows Christ embracing a local saint; presenting him as a patron and father he draws the worshipper into a tripartite conversation.

In the fourth century a defence of images as the *biblia pauperum*, the Bible of the unlearned, began to receive theological formulation. Yet ironically enough, it was just about this time that the use of images ceased to be confined to the didactic. Images were coming to serve as a focus for prayer and devotion, a part which had an increasingly prominent place in the texture of Christian living after the time of the emperor Justinian in the sixth century.[15] At the end of the fourth century, making the gesture of *proskunesis*, prostration, before the cross was assumed to be the most natural Christian behaviour.[16] In Hypatius of Ephesus, rather more than a century later, we have our first literary witness to a similar gesture before the images.[17] Seventh-century saints' lives tell of the cult of the images of Christ, Mary, and the saints in ordinary households.[18] In the same period, the veneration of images began to be part of the Church's public liturgy as texts associated with the great Byzantine theologian Maximus the Confessor testify.[19] The Vienna Codex of John Moschus' *The Meadow*, a monastic anthology of Christian experience, happens to include the story of a dream in which an image of Christ in the city of Antioch was found to be dressed in clothes previously given to a beggar. Such a dream seems to hint at an important intuition of popular Christian piety in the age of the Fathers, namely, that in some sense the reality of God in Christ is disclosed in the image.

We may allow that many factors extrinsic to the revelatory qualities of the art of basilica, catacomb, and portrait played their part in this upsurge of enthusiasm for images. The cult of the holy man and in particular the desire for a person-to-person relation with him as one's spiritual father and as an intercessor, may well have been such a factor.[20] So may the veneration of the image of the emperor, for the church authorities had withdrawn their opposition to such practices when the Basileus belonged to the Christian empire and accepted the subordination of the *polis* to a greater providence which Christianity taught.[21] And so, finally, may the cult of relics.[22] In a lyrical passage of his *Encomium on St Theodore* the Cappadocian church father Gregory oᶠ Nyssa, writing in the fourth century, refers to relics as a material contact whereby we can 'embrace the living body in its full flower'.[23] If such a perception of the Christian saints was being sought, then evidently the work of the painter could be of greater assistance to the imagination than could a handful of bones and dust. Since according to a patristic adage *gloria Dei vivens homo*, 'the glory of God is beheld in man fully alive', then the artistic rendering of the living form of the saint would predictably inherit the significance bestowed on the relic and eventually surpass it. But in the last resort the expectations Christians came to acquire of the art image belonged to the deep internal structure of the Christian faith. Weaving through all the evidence we have just reviewed is the thread of a theme which binds together the first creation of Christian icons and their later veneration: the desire to recognize and experience the presence of God in Christ and his saints. The icon proved the disclosure of this possibility because, as we have seen in our analysis of Paul's theology, God has made himself portrayable in the humanity of Jesus and his faithful disciples. So the image offers the believer an experience of salvation, in the sense that of its very nature it witnesses to God's drawing near in self-communication to man.

People in the early Church found the artistic image important enough to care to think out some account of how it communicates divine meanings. Sometimes, but not always, these first modest steps towards an aesthetic theory were taken in defence of the images against Jewish, or anti-iconic Christian, opponents. We have noted that scholars over the last hundred years have tended to exaggerate the degree of hostility shown to art in the Church of the Fathers. This misapprehension has been reflected in the composition of iconoclastic *florilegia*, handed down from scholar to scholar, where patristic references to idolatry are tied down to matters of art and Christian worship. The following passage, for instance, occurs either *in toto* or by allusion in most erudite accounts of art in the early Church:

> I came to a village called Anablatha, and, as I was passing, saw a lamp burning there. Asking what place it was and learning it to be a church, I went in to pray, and found there a curtain hanging on the doors of the said church, dyed and embroidered. It bore an image either of Christ or of one of the saints; I do not rightly remember whose the image was. Seeing this, and being loth that an image of a man should be hung up in Christ's church contrary to the teaching of the Scriptures, I tore it asunder and advised the custodians of the place to use it as a winding sheet for some poor person.

This autobiographical narrative comes from the pen of the Cypriot bishop Epiphanius of Salamis and describes an event during his tour of Palestine towards the end of the fourth century. The translation is of the Latin version of the *Letter to John of Jerusalem* in which the passage occurs. Sister Charles Murray, of the Sisters of Notre Dame, has shown that in the Greek text of the *Letter* Epiphanius writes of not an icon but 'an idol in the shape of a man', *androeikelon ti eidoloeides*, alleged to represent Christ or a saint by the bystanders, not by the bishop himself. Similarly, the Latin text refers to the authority of Scripture forbidding human representation, while the Greek original simply says that idolatry is hateful to the Church. As a preacher in the image-filled church of the Anastasis in Jerusalem and a friend of pope Damasus, the patron of the Christian monuments in Rome, it seems unthinkable that Epiphanius was the ferocious Iconoclast *avant la lettre* he has been made

55

out to be. Certainly he would have made a poor guest in the papal *familia* for, as Sister Charles remarks, Sunday walks through the Catacombs with their painted decorations, so conducive to meditation, were a favourite form of recreation for the Roman Christians of this pontificate. Yet as we shall see from Eusebius of Caesarea, that influential and established imperial theologian of the same century, there was genuine conflict over the legitimacy of images in the patristic epoch. We may take such conflict as an important part of the background to the beginnings of an apologia for art in the Church.[24]

The earliest attempts to offer a philosophy for the images, those of the fourth century, urge that they should be seen as a kind of Christian pedagogy for passing on the truths of the faith. We find this in the East, with the Cappadocian fathers, and in the West, with the Romano-Gallic patrician figure of Paulinus of Nola whose ministry straddled France and Italy and the fourth and fifth centuries. In the words of Basil the Great, 'What the verbal account presents to the ear the silent picture reveals by imitation'. The image is, in Gregory of Nyssa's phrase, a 'language-bearing book'.[25] Paulinus covered the walls of his basilica with sacred pictures, he tells us, so that 'the forms and colours might seize upon the astonished minds of the country folk' and make them 'feed with their eyes instead of their lips'.[26] The stress may be on the nourishment the mind finds in art or on moral education or, as in Paulinus with his hint of an ascetic distaste at the social habits of the peasantry on pilgrimage, it may be on both of these together. It was on such pragmatic grounds and by means of a correspondingly simple didactic aesthetic that pope Gregory the Great in the sixth century was to defend church art against the Western Iconoclast Serenus of Marseilles.[27]

In his oration *On the Godhead of the Son and of the Holy Spirit* Gregory of Nyssa edged perceptibly away from this view of art as useful for educators towards a concept of the artwork as a vehicle for Christian prayer, a medium for deep emotional experience. This is how he sees an image of the Sacrifice of Isaac known to him.[28] The fifth-century historian Philostorgus in his *Church History* remarks that in the man who lingers with joy over an image of Christ we see a demonstration of love for the figure portrayed there.[29] There is also a splendid dialogue in very much these same

56

terms in the *Quaestiones ad Antiochum Ducem* where an unknown early Christian author defends the veneration of images by saying:

> We make an obeisance to express the attitude and love of our souls for those represented in the icon ... to show our longing for them, just as we do in greeting our fathers and our friends.[30]

A further step was taken with the notion of *anagoge*, ascent, introduced by the theologian who worked under the pseudonym of 'Denys the Areopagite'.[31] His account of how the spirit of man 'rises up' by symbols and images to a deeper penetration of the meaning of the economy of God's salvation was not concerned explicitly with the artwork but the application to art seemed obvious to some people at least in the Great Church. Hypatius of Ephesus, writing to his suffragan Julian of Atramytion in the early sixth century explains the anagogic capacities of the artwork:

> We conceive that each order of the faithful is guided and led up to the divine in its own fashion, and that some are led up material decorations towards the Intelligible Beauty, and from the abundant light in the sanctuaries to the Intelligible and Immaterial Light.[32]

The presence of Denys' vocabulary, profoundly marked by the thought-world of the neo-Platonist philosophers as this was, is quite striking in this passage. As we read on, however, we find it used in the service of a thoroughly biblical theme, the divine *katabasis*, condescension towards man, which grounds the *anabasis*, ascent, of believers into God's presence. For, in Hypatius' view, the primary subject glorified in the holy images is 'the indescribable and incomprehensible philanthropy of God towards us'. But for the author, as this text implies, images exist in the Church by way of a gracious concession to weaker brethren who need such props to the life of faith. It has been suggested that episcopal attitudes of this kind in Asia Minor may have persisted till later, and would thus go far in explaining the activity of the bishops of the region against the cult of images when the Iconoclast crisis at last broke upon the Greek Church.[33] Here in Hypatius, as subsequently in other disciples of Denys such as John Damascene,[34] we find a line of defence of the images that draws on the metaphysical notion of *eikon* so wide-spread in Hellenistic patterns of thought. This idea of the expression or manifestation of one level of being in another, useful though it was to prove in saving visual art from those who would have chased it out of the Church, was on the whole an obstacle to the making of a satisfactory aesthetic theology. It displaced an aesthetic term from its proper context, that of art, to the context of philosophical cosmology. That is not a disadvantage for philosophy since all metaphysics requires the extension of language into analogy. But when in the controversy over the icons the cosmological notion of the image was transferred once again to art it had lost on the way an absolutely vital element of all aesthetics. It allowed nothing for the active role of the perceiver in aesthetically communicated meaning, whether that perceiver be the artist himself or his audience. The account of the descent of the divine energies in Denys already carries, perhaps, the root mistake. It is possible, unfortunately, to describe God's self-communication to man in a way which largely ignores the element of creaturely response and co-operation. The theological theme of God's self-communication in his image man, and of the interpretation of that self-disclosure in that human image by means of art requires a subtle handling of the relation between creaturely structures of being and the divine act. Denys' work does not possess this subtlety and from it could be drawn a unilateral picture of divine revelation, the natural aesthetic for a Christian of Monophysite tendencies who would see the integrity of Christ's humanity subsumed under the divine.

When we reach the late sixth century, we encounter a defence of the images in terms of the theology of the Priestly Writing, seen across that creative rupture in Judaism which Jesus had brought. Not surprisingly, it takes place in Alexandria where highly cultured communities of Christians and Jews lived cheek by jowl. From John Moschus we learn of a learned scholastic of the city, one Cosmas, whom John visited on sorties of book-borrowing and constantly found engaged in reading to prepare for discussion with his Jewish friends. We are fortunate to have a text which seems to be the record of one such dialogue. A Christian writer who made long stays in Egypt, Leontius of Neapolis, grounds the veneration of images on Genesis 1.

The image of God is man, especially that man who has received the indwelling of the Holy Spirit. Justly, therefore, do I honour and worship the image of God's servants and glorify the house of the Holy Spirit.[35]

Interestingly enough, this seems to involve a return to one patristic reading of Genesis which we shall consider in the next section when we turn to look at the theology of the Fathers. Irenaeus of Lyons had seen the image as most importantly including man's bodiliness: imagehood of God belongs, or rather is meant to belong, to the whole form of man's incarnate existence. Leontius' text is one of those that draws on a thread in the huge patristic corpus of teaching on 'Man in the Image of God' that is closely relevant to the model of the artwork because it takes seriously the *embodied* character of man's condition and communication.

Finally, what will become the classic christological argument for the image is already being aired in this early period. George Pisides extolled the image of Christ known as 'The Camuliana' (it was brought to the capital from Cappadocia under the emperor Justin II in the 570s) because it is a tangible witness to the Incarnation of God in Christ's humanity, a 'new Bethlehem'.[36] In a sermon attributed to Gregory Nazianzen, the image is interpreted as a kind of re-enactment of the Incarnation. Since the Word Incarnate is himself in the nature of an image, appealing to 2 Corinthians, his image shares in the character of an incarnation.[37] Similarly, the Council *in Trullo* in 692 saw the image as a challenge to christological heretics: its Christian point lies in its power to make palpable the Incarnation of the Logos in Christ. In the doctrinal programme given by this council, the artistic practice and image theology of the Byzantine Church were authoritatively commended. The tentative approach to the image in the first centuries gives way henceforth to a new confidence. Interestingly, the symbolizing of Christ as the Lamb of the Old Testament is forbidden. The council fathers speak of it as a kind of image which belongs to the world of 'types' and 'shadows' that preceded the fulness of grace and truth that Jesus showed forth. They prescribe, therefore, that Christ should be depicted instead in his humanity, which is the image of that fulness.

On certain paintings one finds the Lamb identified by the pointing finger of the Precursor, placed there as a type of grace, allowing us a preview, through the Law, of the true Lamb, Christ our God. While we honour the types and shadows as symbols of the truth, figures sketched for the benefit of the Church, we prefer to these the grace and truth received as the fulfilment of that Law. We decree therefore that henceforth this fulfilment will be represented before the eyes of all in paintings. He who has taken away the sin of the world, Christ our God, will be portrayed in the icons according to his human character, in place of the ancient lamb. Through this portrayal we realize the height of the humiliation of God the Word and are led to remember his life in the flesh, his suffering and his saving death, and the redemption that issued from it for the world.[38]

Soundings in the Fathers

In this section we shall look at the christological application of the theme of the image of God in the work of the great Fathers of the Eastern tradition. We have just noted how art and christology were beginning to touch each other in the minds of Byzantine people in the sixth century. By the eighth century, when the struggle over the icons commenced, the inter-connections and mutual implications of attitudes to the visual image and attitudes to Christ as the embodied image of God were evident and inescapable.

The comments of the Fathers on the theme of the image are ample enought. Indeed, several individual Fathers have been made the subjects of sizeable and magisterial monographs by modern patristic scholars.[39] But not all by any means of this material is immediately germane. Some theologies of the image in the patristic Church have cut their moorings from the initial metaphor of the artwork so effectively that they have nothing direct to contribute to the approach of this essay. Yet even the most spiritualized accounts of the image have a certain oblique value, as we shall see when we turn to the relation of the model of the artwork to the theology of faith, the subjective aspect of the theology of revelation. The task of connecting the Image christology of the Fathers and visual art is at best elusive, for these theologians were working at the very beginnings of Christian art before it had really become a subject for theological reflection. Without the backdrop of the high patristic writing on Christ the Image, however, it is doubtful whether the Iconophile theologians of the eighth and ninth centuries would have managed to vindicate the icons before the bar of theological reason. This does not mean that the traffic was all one way, from christology to art. G. B. Ladner simplifies excessively when he claims that 'the Greek Christian concept of the image was elaborated not in the sphere of art but in close contact with the development of the most fundamental dogmas about God and man'.[40] The image language used in the formulation of christological doctrine drew not only on the deep roots of the Genesis metaphor of the cultic image but also on the understanding of the image in the art of the Hellenistic world. There was, in other words, a rich plurality of sources feeding the metaphor of the artwork. In particular, sources of meaning feeding the metaphor from an awareness, however limited, of the character of art joined in confluence with sources of meaning issuing from the delineation of God and man in the dogmatic tradition.

We may start with a Father who absorbed little of the philosophical heritage of the Greek world but who has nevertheless been dubbed 'the first great catholic theologian',[41] doubtless for his remarkably unified vision of Christian faith. Unity was the great passion of *St Irenaeus*, born in Smyrna in Asia Minor around 130 and dying towards the year 200, probably as a martyr, at the other end of the Christian *oikoumene*, at Lyons where he had become bishop about 178. His concern for unity was not only a defence of the single apostolic tradition of the Church against the multitude of sectarian schools. It was also an affirmation of the unity of God the Creator and God the Redeemer, and, most importantly, of the unity of spirit and flesh in man. Irenaeus' theological teaching in his *Contra Haereses* takes as its overriding objective the refutation of the fully-fledged Gnostic system which had grown up under the inspiration of the presbyter Valentinus. Although his writing has this strongly marked apologetic character it is marked by a fine grasp of the biblical outlines of the Christian mystery.[42] The Gnosticism he was combating harboured a profound distrust of the material embodiment of the human spirit. It saw that spirit as estranged from the empirical world in which man could in no sense hope to find himself at home.[43] The divine image in Genesis, accord-

61

ing to the Gnostics, could not belong to man as taken from the dust of the earth. The 'earth' of the Bible could only be metaphorical for some ideal and invisible world-stuff which the Demiurge or Creator was said to animate.[44] When Irenaeus treats of man in his perfected condition, man as he was meant to be, he reacts in the strongest way against this teaching. Even if we distinguish the 'soul which takes to itself the Spirit of the Father' and 'the flesh of man' we should still see this latter as formed after the image of God, *plasmata secundum imaginem*.[45] In a later passage of the *Contra Haereses* he speaks more inclusively. The 'image of God' is a condition of the whole of human nature, spiritual and bodily in one. The Logos in becoming incarnate in Jesus Christ became the whole of that nature which was his image.[46]

The master-theme of Irenaeus' theology is *recapitulatio*, a theme with a remarkable number of embodiments in his writing. It means variously restoration, identity of experience, transformation, consummation, all diverse but related variations on a single theological melodic line. One important way of expounding Christ as the recapitulator of mankind is to say that the incarnation was the exhibition of the image in which man was originally made. Man's original capacity for Godshapedness, his initial capability of acting as a disclosure of God, was restored to him in the person of Jesus. In Christ, that is, we discern a revelation of the divine in the human which we somehow recognize, for it holds out to us a condition of life which far from being alien to us answers to our deepest desires. But when Irenaeus turns to speak about the doctrine of man *ex professo* he at once modifies this assertion. His concept of Adam the child implies that man in his beginnings was immature man. Adam possessed the image and likeness of God only in a weak sense, which excludes our saying that humanity in him was full or perfect humanity. At one point he goes so far as to set a query against the obvious sense of Genesis:

> In times long past it was said that man was created after the image of God. But this image was not actually shown. The Word, after whose image man was created, was as yet invisible. . . . When, however, the Word of God became flesh he confirmed both the image and the likeness. For he showed forth the image . . . and the likeness he re-established unshakeably by assimilat-

ing man to the invisible Father by means of the visible Word, *Verbum visibile.*[47]

Irenaeus wants to maintain, then, a highly nuanced position on Jesus and the image of God in man. Christ is God's image, disclosing him to men, through the power he has to focus in himself a whole history of partial disclosures of the divine in men while at the same time bringing that history to a hitherto unheard-of completion. As the second Adam Christ sums up in his own person the whole sequence of man's experience of the divine, thereby hallowing it. At the same time he also inaugurates a quite new humanity. Irenaeus holds in tension a sense of the continuity of the living, human 'imagery' of revelation, as in the prophets, with the idea that there is an extraordinary novelty in the expression of God in human terms which is Jesus Christ. Although Irenaeus loves the thought of human evolution, of growth into perfection, he nowhere draws the conclusion that Christ is simply the crown of human development, the perfect man in whom the Logos was fully revealed, wholly in series with previous revelations. But if the disclosure of God in Christ is truly anticipated in the prophets he is obliged to ask himself, 'What, then, did the Lord bring to us by his advent?' The answer he gives is a striking one. 'Know that he brought all novelty by bringing *himself* who had been announced!'[48]

Travelling east and south from the world of Irenaeus we would strike the Alexandria of *Clement* and *Origen*. Here we encounter a different style of theology, forged in the catechetical school of Alexandria with its openness to the lively philosophical culture of Greek-speaking Egypt.[49] More missionary-minded, certainly more intellectually respectable within the culture of its day, the School lacked by the same token the Christian balance of Irenaeus with his more exclusive dependence on Scripture read within the living tradition of the Church. Clement, born in the middle years of the second century, had spoken in his miscellaneous collection of *aperçus*, called the *Stromateis* or *Carpets* from its winding threads of arguments, of the visibility of God in Christ. The incarnation is the Son's step into the range of the visible.[50] Clement responds to the event in a splendid piece of lyrical writing which explores a metaphor of light. The incarnation is the rising of a new sun on the world, the revelation of the Father which alone brings us the true light of the knowledge of God.[51] This becoming visible of the Word is a sensuous affair, and the senses, correspondingly, are vitally operative in perceiving it.[52] Yet at other moments Clement sees the divine Word not as the depth of divine significance in the visible humanity of Jesus but in competition with that humanity, preferring to think of the Logos as the true 'inner man' in Christ.[53] Clement passed on this hesitation about the unity of form and content, visual image and significance, in Jesus to his remarkable successor, Origen.

An Eastern Orthodox church historian, George Florovsky, and a Dominican patrologist, Christoph von Schönborn, have concurred in tracing to Origen's teaching the 'model for a theology which will lead to Iconoclasm'.[54] For Origen it is, paradoxically, the pre-existent *invisible* Son who is the primary image of the Father, not the Word made flesh.[55] He tends to see the incarnation as a divine pedagogy, rather than as the enduring form of God's presence in the time that follows on from Jesus. His ideal of the knowledge of God in Christ is seeing the Logos 'naked', without its vesture of flesh. The bodily medium of revelation, however necessary in God's relations with man, is, for this Father, an area of ambiguity. He betrays an embarrassment, which would dog Christian theology at many points in the future, about a revelation which takes place through the contingent, through a particular configuration of matter. Origen's comments on the verb 'to see' and its cognates in the Fourth Gospel strongly suggest that for him Jesus is contemplated as the revelatory form of the divine Word in the sense that he provides occasions for vision, rather than being in his very physicality the medium of presentation through which the reality of God is communicated.[56] In his biblical exegesis he stresses the need to press on beyond a 'bodily' sense of Scripture to reach the gospel that is spiritual and eternal.[57] It is in harmony with all of this that in a passage of his debate with a cultivated non-Christian philosopher, the *Contra Celsum*, he frames a direct contrast between the 'dead' images of the pagans with the true 'images' of God, the souls of Christians who carry interiorly the beauty of divine virtues.[58]

Origen's theology is not wholly, however, a desert of aridity for an aesthetic theology. His cursory treatment of the significance of the visibility of revelation derives partly from the fact that he is not concerned with the 'how' of revelation in Christ but with the 'what' of the end and purpose of this revelation, the mystical union of the soul with the hidden God and the union in knowledge and love between the Church and God.[59] Still, the 'ascent' from the visible humanity of Jesus to the God who expresses himself by uniting his Word with Christ's human soul is always for Origen dependent on the once-and-for-all event of the tangible coming of the Son into the flesh. As Father Alois Grillmeier has put it,

> Even if the corporeality of Christ has in some respects the more negative function of a filter and appears to lose its significance as a medium of revelation in the vision of eternity, nevertheless the whole possibility of this vision and the ascent to it depend, even in Origen, on the fact of the Incarnation.[60]

More positively and more originally, Origen offers a valuable concept, that of the *epinoiai* or 'aspects' of Christ, for the increasingly full ways in which the visible humanity of Jesus can be 'read' as you move by way of him towards the invisible God.[61] Origen believed that the signifiance of Jesus can never be tied down to a single lapidary statement. The figure is never found in monochrome. Instead, living in communion with the face of Jesus, we find that we can see him in different ways, connected by Origen with the New Testament 'titles' of Christ: Word, Son, Lamb, and so forth. This multiplicity, which is already present in the Gospels themselves, reflects not simply our difficulties of perception but something that is true of Jesus in himself. He is rich enough to show different faces to men at different stages on the journey towards God. Nevertheless, there is a definite trajectory along which we must pass if we are to see him progressively more integrally and justly, leading to the point where we find ourselves using for him the title of Logos, the self-expression of God. To travel this road biblical erudition is not enough. We have to be living in faith, by love, and open in prayer to the enlightenment of the Holy Spirit.[62]

Origen's most crucial disciple, in the perspective of the theology of the image, is *Eusebius of Caesarea*, father of church history and counsellor of the emperor Constantine the Great. He was trained in the tradition of Origen by the scholar-martyr Pamphilus, standing therefore two generations from the master. Among the many writings of his eventful public life we have a theological comment

65

on Christian images, produced for the benefit of Constantia, the emperor's sister.[63] Constantia had written to ask her brother's protégé for an icon of Christ, apparently of the kind known to us from the wax-based portable icons at St Catherine's monastery on Mount Sinai. Such an image would attempt to portray Christ's features in an icon which could be carried around while travelling and so venerated at daily prayer. She is rebuked by Eusebius in no uncertain terms. If what she wants is an image of the historical Jesus, as he looked while he lived on earth, not only is such a thing forbidden by the second commandment but there are simply no examples to be found. If what she wants is an image of Jesus in the glory of his Father's life, of the exalted Christ, then there is a rather more complex theological objection which she should note. When Christ's humanity became transparent to the invisible Godhead 'the flesh was so mingled with the glory of the divinity that the mortal part was swallowed up by (the divine) Life even when he was on earth'. Eusebius refers to the episode of the Transfiguration. How could it be possible to represent the transfigured countenance of Jesus 'when even the super-human disciples could not bear the sight'? Clearly, the incarnate form of Christ would be even less susceptible to painting after the Resurrection. The form of a slave that Christ assumed is now 'totally transformed', Eusebius says, in the indescribable light of the Word. 'How should one paint the image of so wonderful and incomparable a form, if indeed one can still call "form" the divine intelligible essence?'

This reply gives away a christology which has carried to an extreme what was merely a tendency in Origen. The title 'Image of God' marks out, in Eusebius' eyes, the inferiority of the Logos, as indeed it can only do when read in the ontological terms characteristic of Hellenistic philosophy.[64] It is in line with this that Eusebius sees the divine Logos as the first 'emanation' from the 'Monad', the Father, very much as later Platonist metaphysics conceived the relation to the One of the Forms of the finite world.[65] For Eusebius, Christ the Image is essentially an instrument, *organon*, of his Father rather than the 'immediator' of his presence.[66] He thinks that perfect Christians need only relate themselves to the Logos, the divine reality in Christ. Not for them any concern with his mere flesh, his visible activity. He describes the passion of Christ as 'merely the act of the human instrument employed by the

Logos'.[67] He wrote in his treatise 'On the manifestation of God', *the Theophania*:

> Since it was necessary that the mortal instrument (the body) should find an end worthy of God after the service it rendered to the Logos it was given it to die . . . the Logos who gives life to all willed to show that the mortal instrument which he used for man's salvation was superior to death, and that it communicated in his own life and universality.[68]

To demonstrate his point, at Easter God raised it to new life. The value of the incarnation for Eusebius is, apparently, purely ethical and didactic. The Logos does not really belong with the flesh wherein he was disclosed. He simply uses a body in order to instruct us about faith and morals. Eusebius has enfeebled very woefully that central theme of New Testament teaching which we explored in Paul, and noted in John and the Writer to the Hebrews, that by disclosing God in the form of his materially embodied existence Christ has brought us into a new kind of communication with the Father.

If Eusebius has a fine sense of the mystery of the spirit of man he is much less aware of how that abyss of the interior life, in the hidden roots of knowing and loving, can be embodied and reflected in a visible form of life, and hence in the images of that form in art.

> It seems to me right to say that the reasonable and immortal soul and the impassible spirit (*nous*) are what preserve in human nature the image and likeness of God. This is so inasmuch as the soul is immaterial, incorporeal, intelligible, reasonable and capable of virtue and wisdom. If anyone knew how to depict in an icon the image (*agalma*) or form (*morphe*) of the soul he would indeed be well placed to do so in respect of even more exalted being.[69]

Eusebius intends this as an *a fortiori* argument, from one degree of improbability to another. In his *Church History* he assumes that a statue of Jesus and the Woman with a haemorrhage which he knows of must be pagan workmanship.[70] Understandably, since for him what the Christian is seeking to know is Christ as divine, not in his humanity. For that the only assistance we need is purity of heart, by which we come to recognize the invisible image of the invisible Father.[71]

If it is true of the evolution of Christian doctrine in general that the flaws Origen's theological synthesis left were painstakingly corrected by the *Cappadocian Fathers* it is certainly true of the theology of the image in particular. Origen's Image christology, so it emerges as Eusebius brings that christology into sharper relief, is defective on two grounds. First of all, it cuts away the necessary grounds for apprehending God in Christ by its offhand treatment of the bodiliness of Christ, preferring to see his status as God's icon in his pre-existent being in God. Secondly, accepting the Son as the image of the Father it works with the concept of image in a way strongly influenced by the common cosmological notion of Hellenism that the image is the manifestation of a superior in an inferior level of reality. Thereby, Origen's teaching threatened to insinuate into the Church belief in some kind of demi-god between God and man. This was the challenge met by the Cappadocian fathers, a group of theologians in the Asia Minor of the late fourth century. Two of them brothers and all three close friends, St Basil, St Gregory of Nyssa, and St Gregory Nazianzen worked in the years after the Council of Nicaea to purify the language of the Christian tribe. They did so by means of a rather austere metaphysical enquiry, but this was animated throughout by a living grasp of the Christian reality they dealt with daily as pastors and as monks.

The Cappadocians' contribution centres on the idea of *hypostasis* or personal subject. Amidst the confusion of thought and language in the years following Nicaea they set out to show the logical sense of the New Testament affirmation that the person of Jesus is the perfect image of God. Basil, in a lengthy letter (the fourth century was an age when personal correspondence could be unblushingly theological) introduces the notion of *hypostasis* to express 'whatever delimits and circumscribes the undetermined being (*phusis*) of some reality'. In speaking of personal subjects, as the very grammar of human language requires us to do, we are talking about whatever makes nature particular and distinctive, as that is known through someone's behaviour or visible characteristics, *epiphainomenon idiomaton*.[72] Now in Christian experience, and here Basil is thinking of both the New Testament and the continuing life of faith in the

Church, these manifest characteristics of the Son and of the Holy Spirit lie in their consistent tendency to exhibit what is other than themselves. The Spirit shows forth the Son; the Son points to the Father. In the case of Jesus, then, at the precise moment when we register something quite distinctive and personalizing about him we also recognize that, uniquely and paradoxically, this something is not his own but consists in sheer relationship to someone other than himself. These somewhat glacial yet serviceable categories provide a basis for the reasonable man to explore a little further how Jesus may be said to be the image of God.

Basil carries forward the discussion in dependence on a text from the Letter to the Hebrews. Jesus Christ is 'the radiant light of God's glory and the very image (*charakter*) of his nature'.[73] Whether the Writer to the Hebrews in fact envisages the pre-existent Christ here rather than the Word Incarnate does not affect Basil's use of his letter, because for the Cappadocian bishop the economy of God's self-manifestation in history is axiomatically the translation into another medium of the relations that hold good in his eternal nature. There would simply be no way of speaking about the pre-existent Son unless we were retrojecting into God's eternal life some aspect of what became visible in the earthly life of Jesus. Basil comments on this opening text of Hebrews that 'the image is the same thing as the prototype – even while it is different'.[74] This apparently gnomic saying is the concentration of what Basil wishes to say about Jesus as in the depths of his personal reality utter transparency to the Father and in the contours of his embodied life the medium of presenting to us that same transparency. The categories of Hellenistic metaphysics are here blown wide open by the sheer force of Christian experience. Of course we cannot see traced in the image the Father's own distinctive quality of being what Greek Christian theology called 'unengenderedness', the absolute Source of infinite as well as finite being. Were that the case Father and Son would be in every sense the same reality. Image and prototype are different. But we can recognize the Unengendered Beauty immanent in the Engendered, the Imaged in the Image.[75] In his treatise *On the Holy Spirit* Basil happens to throw out the remark that the honour given to the icon passes to the prototype.[76] It would become in time a *locus classicus* for the Byzantine Iconophiles. But what really counts for the art of God incarnate in Basil's teaching is not this aside on

69

the philosophy of art so much as his reflection on the personal relationships of Father, Son, and Holy Spirit. Following his lead the word *prosopon*, used interchangeably with *hypostasis* for the unique configuration of characteristics proper to a subject, comes to be employed for Jesus as the face of God in the most significant possible sense. The theatrical overtones of masks and greasepaint which the word carried in secular Greek usage fall away and are replaced by fresh connotations in a re-worked language suited to the description of personal disclosure.

St Gregory of Nyssa, taking up this teaching in his battle with the Eunomians over the Son's freedom, translates it into terms of the gospel narrative about Jesus' actions. He writes in his first *Treatise against Eunomius*, 'It is not possible to recognise the archetypal Good except when he appears in the image of what is invisible.' This image is glimpsed in the form of life which Jesus' characteristic activity showed forth. 'He appears as the image, seal, shadow and radiance of the Prototype by the wonderful quality of his deeds'.[77] The son's specific 'manner of subsisting', *tropos tes huparcheos*, is existence as the obedient and loving Person who makes visible the Father's goodness. His obedience becomes the image of the Father since he assumes into his own filial existence the whole of the Father's will to the point where his existence is simply identified with that will. 'He was the very willing of the Father'.[78]

In 412 a passionate, authoritarian but skilful and precise theologian succeeded his uncle in the patriarchal see of the city where Clement and Origen had worked. *St Cyril of Alexandria* fought for much of his life against the Eusebian incubus in christology. In his own time that particular branch in the genealogical tree of patristic theology had brought forth its last bitter fruit in the Nestorian conviction that the flesh of Christ, now conceived as the 'mere man', is essentially external to the Logos. Cyril appeals 'abundantly'[79] to the metaphor of the image in expounding his own counter-teaching that God is now present to us by an indissoluble union of the Logos with our flesh.

In his essay on the unity of Christ, *Quod unus sit Christus*, Cyril teaches that the divine Word 'took to the form of a slave not by adding to himself a man, as the Nestorians would have it, but by taking to himself this *form (eidos)* while remaining in the likeness

70

of his Father.[80] As Père M. de Durand, O. P., summarizes Cyril's doctrine in this text, the incarnation for Cyril is essentially 'the permanent stratagem which allows God to become visible and palpable among us'.[81] Cyril's instence on the bodily medium of divine revelation is so marked that he actually prefers to speak of *sarkosis*, becoming flesh, while pointing out from time to time that this must mean *enanthropesis*, becoming man. This follows not from some dithering hesitation as to whether Jesus had a proper human mind and soul but from a clear anthropological option. For Cyril soul is an attribute of the flesh: it is what raises flesh up to life and intelligence. Man is an animated body rather than an embodied soul. In his *Scholia de incarnatione Unigeniti* the humanity of Christ is likened to the wood of the Ark of the Covenant.[82] The body is the outward face, the soul the inward surface of the Ark; and both are gilded by the divine presence. He represents the Word as stooping to take possession firstly of the flesh of man, and only thus entering the realm of the human soul. Christ's soul cannot be referred to except as the soul-of-this-flesh,[83] over which the Word has 'spread the splendour of his glory'.[84] For Cyril the Christian era is essentially a time when God is expressed in the features of a human face. Taking up a phrase of the psalmist about Israel's destiny as 'the day of God's face',[85] Cyril says that

> We can quite justly understand 'the time of the face of the Father' as the era of the incarnation. For truly the Son is the face (*prosopon*) and the image of the Father.[86]

Yet Christ is not God's image simply as 'this flesh' of Jesus in a static sense. He is the Father's image because he has become flesh for our salvation, through what the great patriarch repeatedly calls 'his goodness and lovingkindness towards man'. The flesh of Jesus possesses a certain vector; and its expressive power issues from the tension between its origin and its destiny. The characteristics that make this flesh divinely image-bearing are disclosed in the events of Jesus' ministry. Jesus becomes the image of God for us as he enacts a sustained and freely-chosen self-emptying to the moment of death.

Let us come then, to that accurate and authentic vision of the

71

Father which is the Son. For we see in him the image of the Father if only we will raise the eyes of our minds towards the fulness which is his. God, the Father, is good of his own being. And similarly good is the Son. How could he not be good who has undergone for us such humbling, coming into the world to save sinners and to give his life for them.[87]

In the Coptic and Syro-Malabar churches of the Christian East there is a tradition that it was Cyril of Alexandria who first introduced icons into the liturgy.[88] The folk memory is historically defective, but it carries some shrewd perceptions. For Cyril, either the flesh of Christ expresses the glory of God in a union comparable to that of the artist and his artwork or the divine glory is not expressed in any sense adequate to the veneration of images of God.

Towards the end of his life Cyril turned to attack explicitly the idea that the humanity of Christ is simply God's instrument in the economy of salvation.[89] He was feeling towards some notion of the co-operation or 'synergy' of divine and human, although this is still only inchoate in his writings. Yet it seems clear from what he has to say on the divinization of the Christian believer, where he speaks of the divine image re-established by the Holy Spirit who thereby re-creates us into communion with the Father, that a doctrine faithful to his inspiration would find Christ's capacity to disclose God in the flesh in the communion and thus perfect co-operation of his human will with the divine.[90]

Around 580 the most thorough theological synthesizer of the Byzantine church, St Maximus, known as 'the confessor' was born in Constantinople. Like St Thomas both in his capacity to unify the earlier tradition and in his concern for the integrity of the divine and the human in Christ and in Christian living,[91] Maximus suffered exile and finally mutilation and death in his opposition to Monothelitism, the doctrine of the 'single will' in Christ's personality. According to Maximus, the union involved in the incarnation is such that it fully respects created nature while transposing that nature into a mode of existence which surpasses its own possibilities. This transcendent movement which completes man's nature is defined by Maximus as *charity*. For him, man's capacity to image God turns on his freedom. No freedom, no capacity to disclose the utterly free God.[92] The difference between the divine and the human, the Uncreated and the created, should be an invitation to free *sunergeia*, to co-operation through communion. Man's 'natural will', the nisus towards fulfilment given with human nature, carries man forward into freedom only because its operation presupposes life in God, conformity with that dynamic relation of man to God which the Creator established. With the Fall, however, this difference is perverted into opposition.[93] Man acts now by his 'gnomic will', a willing which derives not from his human nature but from his *hypostasis*, his personal subjectivity which is itself the origin of his revolt against God and against nature. Such a freedom can only be the freedom to destroy oneself. Under such a regime of existence the face of man is disfigured, for the divine image is blurred.[94] Man is folded back on himself, living under a tyranny of self-love. Nothing can free man from this subservience except some intervention which draws on more than his present potentialities, some victory over the perverted dynamism that sustains the opposition to God.

For Maximus this victory is Christ's cross and its power consists in the charity which takes Jesus to Calvary in obedience to the Father. The cross re-establishes the image of God in man not from outside but in and through a human existence, which must mean a human willing and acting. 'For such was the Saviour's aim, to obey his Father till death, precisely as man, for our profit'.[95] Touching on the Agony of Jesus in the Garden of Gethsemane Maximus speaks of Christ showing there how his will was 'marked', *tupoumenos*, by the divine will and how he thus struggled to realize his destiny in an intimate union, *sumphuia*, with that will. Maximus' vocabulary for speaking of this marking of Christ's human will by the divine is an iconographic one, containing as it does such doing words as *tupoo*, to make an impression, form, mould, model, and *schematizo*, to form, shape. In a lyrical outburst in his *Letter* 64 he makes the metaphor of the artwork explicit for this interrelation of the divine and the human achieved in Christ and manifested by him in his deeds.

O most mysterious mystery of them all! God himself has truly become man, through charity taking flesh, mind, and reasonable soul, and assuming into himself without change the passions of nature. This he has done in order to save man and to give himself to us as the impress of virtue, the living icon of charity and goodness.[96]

Maximus sees the Transfiguration of Christ as the paradigm for our perception of the hidden God who yet becomes visible in his living image and Son. Père Alain Riou concludes from his recent study of the little-known passage of the *Ambigua* where Maximus offers his exegesis of the Transfiguration that Maximian christology here prepares the ground for the teaching on Christ and his icons which St Theodore of Studios and others created in the throes of the Iconoclast Controversy.

> The articulation of the visible and the hidden is not expressed through some conceptual connection which links the signifier to some other reality signified. It happens, rather, by the affirmation of their unity in a personal 'himself' (*heautos*), in the single *prosopon*, face and person of the Lord in his two natures, divine and human. Like the *hypostasis*, the symbolic character of Christ has no independent reality but is simply this transparence of two irreducible modalities of the same subject, this 'love towards man' whereby in the eternal counsel of God and in the accomplishment of that counsel in the flesh, the beloved Son who was obedient unto death accepted until the end that they were united in his person.[97]

We have seen something of the variety of patristic theologies that touch on the theme of the image. The use of image language for Christ as the embodiment and thereby the restoration of true humanity in Irenaeus shows that the roots of the metaphor in sensory visual perception were not forgotten. Eusebius, drawing on the heavily philosophical concept of *eikon* in Origen, is capable of using the concept to diminish both the fulness of the Father's presence in the Son and the continuing significance of Christ's humanity. This unfortunate sub-tradition is consciously combated at Alexandria by Cyril, after the application of the metaphor to the inner-Trinitarian life and the Trinitarian economy in salvation-history has been clarified by the Cappadocians, especially Basil. Finally, in Maximus the Confessor, the model of the artwork is explicitly appealed to in order to show how the transcendent mystery of the

74

Father may be said to be fully expressed in the human existence of the Son, This existence, as face and as a form of life ordered to the cross, the overthrow of all self-love, is manifested in a will which has become so modelled and in-formed by the divine will that the deeds which flow from it may be seen as the graphic illustration of God's love towards man. These are some of the dogmatic uses of the metaphor which will be relevant when the model of the artwork is itself debated as a possible way of speaking about salvation. That debate ran its furious course in the Iconoclast crisis to which we must now turn.

CHAPTER FIVE

The Vindication of the Icons

The moves against the use of icons that began with the accession of the Byzantine emperor Leo III in 714 initiated a major spiritual and cultural crisis within Christendom, as well as a period of political turmoil in the Eastern Roman empire. In the words of the historian of doctrine Jaroslav Pelikan, the debate reached out 'into every aspect of East Roman civilisation, not only into the church but into the court, the academy, the monastery, the artist's studio and the private home'.[1] The factors involved in the struggle for the icons are astonishingly complex: it can be seen as an attempt by the imperial power to reassert its own claims to organize the 'holy' in society, against the local, personal, centrifugal charisms of Byzantine monasticism; it can be seen as the temporary emergence of elements in Byzantine culture that were, if not totally alien, at least provincial or non-Hellenic; and it can be seen in strictly theological terms as 'a debate about the meaning of the incarnation for history, about the definition and interpretation of christian worship and about conflicting claims to the title of the city of God.'[2] The Iconodule teaching that the Iconoclast theologians threw up by way of reaction brought a theology of the artwork and a christology of the image into explicit relation, and so set a target for the attempt to restate an aesthetic christology later in this essay. In this chapter we shall look first at the challenge of the Iconoclasts to the icons in its historical context and then the response that the Iconodule theologians made in defence of Christian art as a way of alluding to God in Christ.

It may be important in trying to understand the origins of Iconoclasm that the emperor Leo III was a man of humble north Syrian background who had risen to prominence as a military administrator in Asia Minor. First, we have seen that some of the bishops of Asia Minor were decidedly cool on the subject of images in the sixth century.[3] Their region had been Leo's home and was the source of an episcopal initiative, from bishop Constantine of Nakoleia, which gave him his opportunity in 726.[4] Second, it may conceivably be the case that an emperor from the oriental marches was more exposed to the influence of those two great anti-iconic traditions, Islam and Orthodox Judaism. The Serbian Byzantinist George Ostrogorsky held that an occupant of the throne who belonged to the Semitic and Caucasian parts of the empire with their non-Greek cultural traditions and their large Monophysite and sectarian communities hostile to the Great Church might well be expected to be unsympathetic to the icons, above all in a period when the challenge of Islam and Judaism were being felt.[5] Three years before the first abortive attack on the images the caliph Yazid II had issued a decree removing representations of living beings from all buildings in his territories, in accordance with the requirements of Koranic law.[6] Is it possible that in a cold war with the Caliphate the eastern-born emperors of the eighth century were concerned to purify Christianity to enable it better to withstand the challenge of Islam? On the role of Judaism the most recent students of Iconoclasm have preferred to speak not of any influence exerted by contemporary Talmudic Judaism but of a renaissance of interest in the Old Testament. In the course of fairly desperate if sporadic military struggles with their neighbours Byzantine people were tending to read their contemporary history with one eye on the parallel of ancient Israel. Professor Peter Brown has written that 'the influence of the Old Testament upon the public image of the Byzantine empire had grown steadily since the reign of Heraclius: the Byzantines were the "true Israel".'[7] He offers the hypothesis that Iconoclasm was an attempt to provide therapy for a corporate anxiety. As city after city fell to the enemy, anxiety about the future was verbalized in the idea that the Byzantine state had drawn down God's wrath by its idolatry in permitting the veneration of the icons. The adoption of this framework did not only help people to take hold of their sense of malaise. It also enabled them to do something about it. As the Old Testament theme of the apostasy, dereliction, and repentance of the people of Israel came alive again, smashing the images could act as a symbol of a new beginning for the empire. But at least as important as any factors of this kind was the theological pressure that bore down on the Byzantine state from the

77

strongly Origenist and anti-iconic churchmen among the imperial advisers.

The crisis proper began with the deposition of the patriarch Germanus of Constantinople in 730 for his defiance of the imperial edict against the icons. If Germanus' own account can be trusted, the imperial decree unleashed a spate of image-breaking and the harassment of unrepentant Iconophiles. The patriarch recorded in his later memoir that the Iconoclasts were not content to do away with panel icons, but also destroyed mural decorations in churches as well as altar covers and reliquaries.[8] The emperor's high reputation for military astuteness and the enduring popularity of Iconoclasm in the hinterland of Asia Minor ensured Leo a solid power-base. This was consolidated, after a brief interlude of unsuccessful usurpation, by his son Constantine V. Constantine was a kind of lay theologian, profoundly and passionately interested in theology and the chief instigator of the synod which, as he saw it, would restore the purity of faith of the apostolic Church by placing Leo's Iconoclast policy on an unshakeable doctrinal foundation.[9] He wrote thirteen theological treatises of which only two have survived, and those in devastated and fragmentary form.[10] These imperial tracts, supplemented as Professor Cyril Mango remarks by a series of 'special lectures', prepared the way for Constantine's council which met in February 754 at Hieria on the Asiatic side of the Bosphorus.[11]

The teaching of the 754 synod and the theological spade-work of Constantine V belong together and are best treated so. The council declared, for instance, what could only have been congenial news to the emperor, that the Iconoclast rulers have resumed the work of the apostles in the Church. The Fathers of the synod aim to co-operate with the emperor in restoring the Church to her original beauty, for she is the immaculate Spouse of Christ who rescued mankind from the worship of idols.[12] They open their fire by describing the abuses to which popular veneration of images has led in East Rome. This documentary serves as a preamble to restating the prohibitions of images in the Old Law. It was generally admitted, however, that the Iconodules themselves recognized and preached against notorious abuses in popular piety, so this line of argument by itself was insufficient for their purposes. Further, the imperial policy was never one of systematic aniconicism since the government went out of its way to encourage a renaissance of secular art to take the place of the icons. The question, then, was how to discriminate between acceptable and unacceptable art. In the reign of the emperor's father an inscription had been placed over the celebrated Gate of Bronze in Constantinople in place of an icon of Christ removed by edict. Dead matter can play no part, it read, in worshipping in spirit and in truth.

> The Lord does not allow that one depict Christ in a portrait that is without voice, deprived of breath, made of earthly matter such as is scorned in the Scriptures. And so Leo, with his son the new Constantine, engraves on the gates of kings the blessed type of the Cross, the glory of the faithful.[13]

Secular art and conventional symbols for Christianity might pass, for these made no attempt to disclose the divine. By contrast the synod anathematizes those who try to convey the form of God's holy ones 'in inanimate, dumb images, made of dead colours, which bring no profit'.[14] The chasm between the image and what it claims to show forth is immeasurable. Material colours are incapable of seizing the glory of the Age to Come. Only the eyes of the mind can grasp that. It may be that there are links here with the theology of contemplation found in the Origenist monk Evagrius of Pontus who located 'pure' prayer in an ascent of the intellect, free of all images, to the invisible God.

In matters of Christology both Constantine V and the bishops of the synod set out to sunder art from the doctrine of the Church about the person of Jesus. The emperor's writings show distinct Monophysite tendencies. The single *prosopon* of Christ is drawn from, *ek*, two natures but after the union these are no longer distinguishable. One of these natures, the divine, cannot be portrayed of its very essence. For this reason the person of Christ, his *prosopon*, cannot be depicted either. Christian artists flounder between the Scylla and Charybdis of two heresies, equally unpleasant. If they want to preserve the unity of Christ then they 'necessarily circumscribe the Word made flesh'. That is, they limit the unlimitable mystery of God himself. If they say that the flesh of Christ has its own distinct face, *prosopon* once more, then they 'make of Christ a mere creature, separating him from the divine Word united with

79

him'.[15] Dr Sebastian Brock, an Oxford Syriac scholar, has shown recently that Monophysite churches in this period were not always aniconic.[16] This does not mean, however, that Monophysitism is not logically aniconic: it is perfectly possible for an individual or a community to miss the logical incoherence between different areas of their belief system. While accepting Constantine's conclusions the synod of 754 subtly modified his premises, perhaps aware of their lack of an orthodox balance. They focus their attention not on the difficult notion of *prosopon* but on the simpler one of the bodiliness of Jesus. The divinization of Christ's flesh by the union with the Word makes all imaging of him impossible. The makers of icons 'separate off the flesh which is interwoven with the Godhead and divinized by it'.[17] As later Iconodules pointed out, this is no more than a camouflage of the Constantinian position, shorn of its dangerous vocabulary. 'To say it is improper for us to see images of Christ is the same as to say it was improper for his disciples to see him. . . . If painting a picture of Christ either confuses his natures or divides them, then the very incarnation itself confused or divided them.'[18]

The synod ended by ordering draconian measures against its opponents, requiring the complete destruction of the icons and excommunicating the leaders of the Iconophile party, who were then abandoned to the mercies of the secular arm. As Cyril Mango has reminded those who accept at face value the somewhat rhetorical statements in the written sources, the *total* destruction of Christian art in the innumerable and often very large churches scattered throughout the Empire was no easy matter, and practical Iconoclasm was in fact far from systematic. Nevertheless the losses were great.[19] In Constantinople itself the representations of the Councils in the Arch of the Milion were taken down and replaced by pictures of chariot races. In the church of the Mother of God at the Blachernae a 'neutral' decoration of vegetal *rinceaux* and birds went up in place of a New Testament cycle. The mosaic of the Virgin in the church of the Dormition at Nicaea was covered over and a plain cross left in its stead. The sharpest opposition came from the monastic world and met with answering persecution. The author of the *Life of St Stephen the Younger* speaks of almost three hundred and fifty monks languishing in the Praetorium prison, and tells us that the only safe refuge for Iconophiles lay in lands where the emperor's jurisdiction could not be effectively enforced, on the northern shore of the Black Sea, the southern shore of Asia Minor, Cyprus, and above all Italy where the monastic clergy in their exodus established a number of Iconophile centres of Greek learning.[20]

The next reign, that of Leo IV, formed a transitional period between the highpoint of Iconoclasm under Constantine and the restoration of the icons under the empress Eirene. Leo's measures against the surviving pockets of Iconodules were of the most moderate, while his widow worked cautiously and diplomatically towards a total *volte-face* of State policy. Her lay secretary, Tarasius, was made patriarch and promptly set about preparations for an Ecumenical Council to reverse the proceedings of 754. The Council met in the church of the Holy Apostles in the capital in the summer of 786, submitting the *Acta* of the Iconoclast synod to a detailed theological critique before it offered its own statement of faith.

> We define with all accuracy and care that the venerable and holy icons be set up like the form of the venerable and life-giving Cross, inasmuch as matter consisting of colours and pebbles and other material is appropriate in the holy Church of God, on sacred vessels and vestments, walls and panels, in houses and on the roads, as well as the images of our Lord and God and Saviour Jesus Christ, of our undefiled Lady, the Holy Mother of God, of the angels worthy of honour and of all holy and pious men. For the more frequently they are seen by means of pictorial representation the more those who behold them are aroused to remember and desire the prototypes and to give them greeting and the worship of honour. . . .[21]

But military collapse under Eirene's successors opened the way for a revival of Iconoclasm, not surprisingly in view of that climate of feeling we have noted, the endemic 'anxiety'. Leo V came from just those Asian circles that were remarkable for men of military ability and of Iconoclast outlook. Convinced that the troubles of the Empire were bound up with the sins of an Iconodule administration Leo commissioned an Iconoclast scholar, John Grammaticus, to stockpile the grapeshot of erudition for another Iconoclast council. The change of government brought the various Iconophile factions together, uniting the more politically conscious moderate group headed by the patriarch Nicephorus with the radical monastic party under Theodore of Studios. From these two men issued a flow of writings in putting the case for the icons and against, incidentally, imperial intervention in matters of faith. Theodore and a number of his followers exiled, Nicephorus deposed, a new synod met at Hagia Sophia in 815 with the way cleared for a repudiation of the Second Counil of Nicaea and the reinstatement of its predecessor of 754. But, as Ostrogorsky wrote, if the Iconoclasm of Leo III and Constantine V was a movement of dynamic vigour the new wave showed all the signs of a merely imitative reaction. In 820 Leo V's life ended in a brutal assassination and a rough but politically adept soldier, Michael II, allowed the Iconodule confessors to return from exile while placing his son and heir Theophilus into the hands of John Grammaticus, for tutorial care. Theophilus' reign, from 829 to 842 was to see the last, especially vicious, gestures of a dying Iconoclasm. The restoration of the images was made possible by revulsion against such policies and carried out, like the first attempt to bring back the icons, under the leadership of a woman. The regent Theodora combined a prudent moderation towards the former adherents of Iconoclasm with a solemn rehabilitation of the holy images in 843.[22] The final rulings of the synod that closed the affair (its full *Acta* are sadly lost) have been taken into the *lex orandi* of the Byzantine Liturgy. They are read every year at the celebration of the Holy Liturgy on the feast of Orthodoxy, the first Sunday of Lent.[23] The spiritual crisis of Byzantium over the artwork had passed away, not without leaving in our possession a treasury of theological literature which we must now examine.

In 725 the leading bishop of Byzantium, *St Germanus*, patriarch of Constantinople, began the theological defence of images in a personal supplication to Leo III. If the emperor were to carry out his projected policy he 'would destroy the divine Economy as that has been given through the flesh'.[24] He wrote in a letter shortly afterwards,

> We feel ourselves urged on to represent what our faith really is, to show that he (the only Son) is not united to our nature in appearance only, in some shadowy way . . . but has become man in reality and in truth. . . . For this reason . . . we represent the

82

character of his holy flesh in the icons, and we venerate and revere them with due honour since they lead us to remember that lifegiving incarnation of his, before which all language must fail.[25]

For Germanus, who proved the soul of resistance to Iconoclasm in the four years left to his patriarchate, the artwork as made and venerated by a Christian is itself the *charakter* of the flesh of Christ. *Charassein* in patristic Greek has the sense both of 'to shape letters' and 'to mark out a form'. Its noun form *charakter* signifies what makes an assemblage of *charagmata*, 'sketchings' into a coherent image. In the memoir he wrote from exile, the *De haeresibus et synodis* Germanus insisted that the making of artworks of the divine is entailed by the incarnation. He equates the 'tradition which we have received of representing Christ in his human form' with the representation of 'his visible *theo*phany'.[26] That is, he placed his finger on the weakest spot of Iconoclast christology, its tendency to see the deification of Christ's humanity as the suppression of its properly human integrity. That humanity was assumed to be in competition with the divine Word rather than, like any created reality, a possible form for God's self-expression.[27]

In *St John Damascene*, the outstanding Greek-speaking theologian of the eighth century (he actually lived in the Caliph's territory, at the monastery of St Sabas near Jerusalem) we find a teaching about the images that is pivoted on the transformation that the relation between God and the world undergoes with the incarnation. In the three orations *On the Holy Icons* which he wrote between 726 and 730 John starts with the affirmation that, by his own will God has become visible, assuming a material existence and conferring on matter a new function and dignity.

Now that God has appeared in the flesh and lived among men, I make an image of the God who can be seen. I do not venerate matter, but I venerate the Creator of matter, who for my sake became material and deigned to dwell in matter, who through matter effected my salvation, . . . matter, filled with divine power and grace.[28]

83

In all of this God has accommodated the means of grace to our human condition.

> Perhaps you are sublime and able to transcend what is material ... but I, since I am a human being and bear a body, want to deal with and behold holy things in a bodily way.[29]

In particular, when Jesus said, 'Blessed are your eyes. . . .' he gave his endorsement to the quest for beatitude through seeing, and therefore to the use of icons as a mediation of that original shewing of himself to his disciples in the scenes of the gospel narratives.[30] Man, structured as he is as a knowing subject in the world, cannot apprehend meanings, *noetika*, without some embodiment of those meanings, *somatika*.[31] This is why the visual image plays such a crucial part in coming to know the divine.[32] John's concept of the image is open in texture. He suggests the following analogically related kinds of image: the archetype of a thing in God's creating mind, the metaphors of Scripture, the adumbrations ('types') of some event that a prior event may contain, man himself, and, not least, the painterly image. This awareness of the analogical character of the concept of the image does not seem to issue, however, in any more rigorous account of the diverse ways in which the divine is reflected. Distinctively aesthetic creation and perception, what actually goes on in the artist's workshop and the believer's icon-corner, tends to disappear into a general metaphysic of reality as opening on to God through 'participation'. The icons, the representations, *charakteres*, of the saints 'share in' the grace and energy of the Holy Spirit.[33] In other words, John assumes here an imaginative structure for perceiving artworks which is not necessarily ours, because it implies what I called in the opening chapter of this book a sense of the world as 'carrying the power and radiance of significant presence', under a law of participation and exchange. Sophisticated societies and primitive societies alike employ both rational or empirical and participatory or mystical modes of thought, as modern anthropologists have been right to insist.[34] Yet neither anthropologists nor theologians are equipped in their professional capacities to trigger a perception of the world as offering the promise of divine presence. If we are to recover John Damascene's sense of the experience of art as somehow continuous with a grasp of the revelation of God in Christ it will not be by rehearsing the neo-Platonist metaphysics on which John, like other disciples of the Areopagite, so heavily relied, but by discovering how artworks can initiate us, through their own aesthetic structure, into a new world of meaning. But this is to anticipate the positive proposals of the last chapters of this essay.

It is in the second Iconoclast period, from 813 onwards, that Iconophile theology really blossoms. *St Nicephorus*, patriarch in these later years, made a radical break with the somewhat cumbersome cosmological aesthetics of late Antiquity by a simple appeal to Aristotle's *Categories*. An image, he said, is a relation, a *pros ti*, a 'being towards' something. 'From the point of view of likeness the icon is both Christ and the image of Christ. It is Christ equivocally, it is Christ's image relatively, *kata to pros ti*.'[35] The aesthetic reality of the icon, as distinct from its merely empirical reality, lies in the relation it sets up towards its subject, an intentional relation or meaning. But can such a relation be established in the case of God in Christ? Constantine V had argued that it could not, but then his argument was merely the assertion of a christological premise which might well be dubious, namely that Christ's humanity was *aperigraptos*, 'uncircumscribed', because of its union with the divine Word. According to Constantine, while the human self-expression of Peter or Paul can be said to be the form that reveals their personhood, this is not the case with Jesus. Nicephorus tackles this premise head-on, making the notion of *perigraphe*, circumscription, the centre-piece of his theological work.

> In Christ human nature is renewed and saved. The body assumed by God is wholly divinized, transformed . . . crowned with indescribable beauty. It becomes Spirit-bearing. It breaks through the heaviness of earthly matter. Very well, yet it does not cease on any of these accounts to be truly body. And if it remains body then it is circumscribed, for that is the very condition, definition, and principle of body.[36]

Divinization is not a de-naturing of nature in Christ. What we contemplate in him is a mortal, corruptible and circumscribed because enfleshed humanity graced with the capacity to live by a

85

divine mode of existence, one which captures in a fresh medium the filial mode of existence of the divine Word.

> The humanity of Christ, if bereft of one of its properties, is a defective nature, and Christ not a perfect man, or rather not Christ at all. He is lost altogether if he cannot be circumscribed and represented in art.[37]

The fullest response to the Iconoclasts is reached not with Nicephorus, however, that 'typical Byzantine patriarch', temperamentally moderate and docile, an emperor's man, but with Theodore of Studios, a monastic reformer and radical with the intransigence of a Becket or a Savonarola. Theodore brought the metaphysical christology of the Greek patristic tradition into the most illuminating relation to theological art that the limitations of its style of reflection would allow. Drawing on the Maximian christology of nature and person Theodore reminds his readers that the hypostatic particularity of Christ, his single *prosopon*, face, bestows its 'common mark', *gnorisma koinon*, on his whole being. Whatever is characteristic of Jesus' humanity is *eo ipso* characteristic of God the Word. The particularity of Jesus' human existence and of the signs that convey that existence to us is what reveals God. And there is no problem about the painterly circumscription of particularities, for it is with particularities that the artist most happily deals.

> In the icon of Christ there is no other hypostasis than that of Christ himself. It is the same hypostasis of Christ, the same character, which appears in the icon in its visible form.[38]

The painterly image is more apt for appreciating and expressing the significance of Jesus than any concepts, not because of any *a priori* superiority in art over against conceptual thought, but because art is more appropriate for an epoch in which the divine is known to have presented itself through the material, the contingent, and the particular. Precisely because we know that, we also know that it will be easier to depict God in Christ than to conceptualize the incarnation.

If (as the Iconoclasts argue) we should perceive him simply with

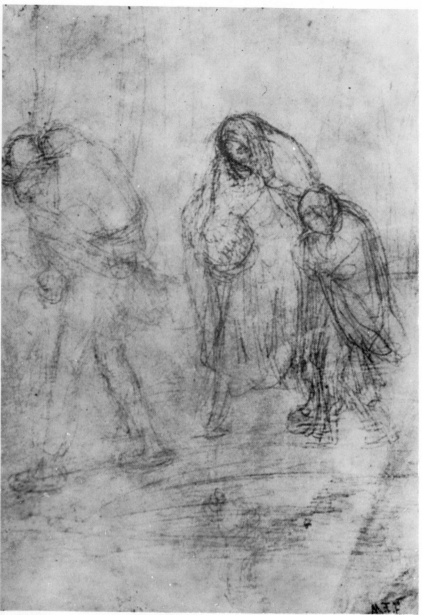

1. L'Arrivée au Barbizon, *Jean Millet*

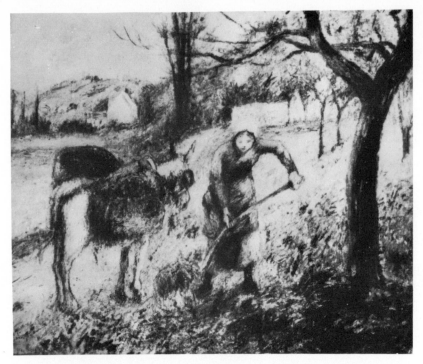

2. Peasant Woman with a Donkey, *Camille Pissarro*

3. The Vision after the Sermon, *Paul Gauguin*

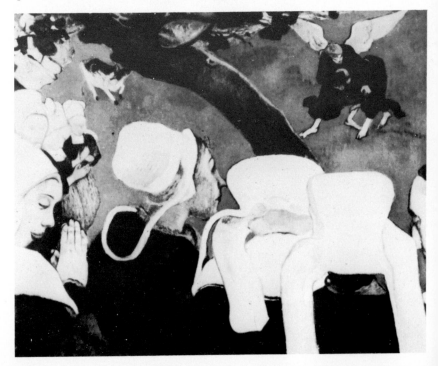

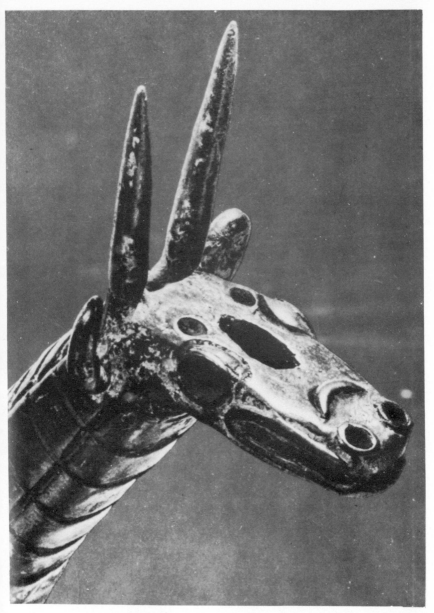

4. The Dragon Head of Marduk

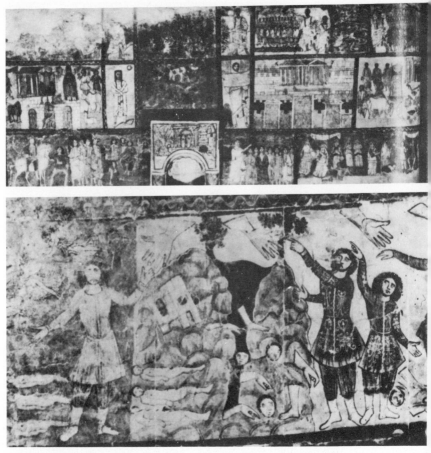

Top 5. The Dura Synagogue: overall view with the Torah Shrine
Middle 6. The Dura Synagogue: the resurrection of Israel before Ezekiel
Below 7. Wall painting of a baptismal scene

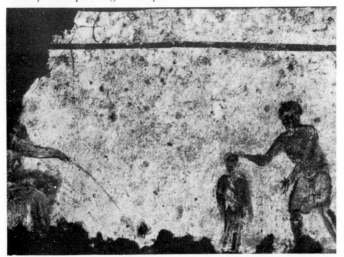

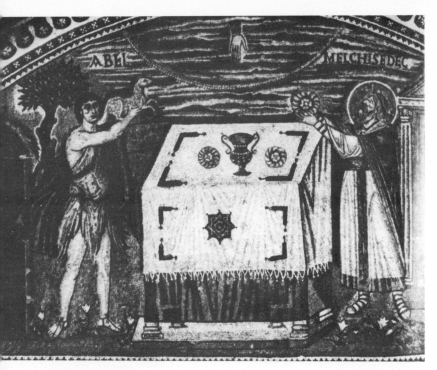

8. Abel and Melchizedek

9. Christ with St Menas

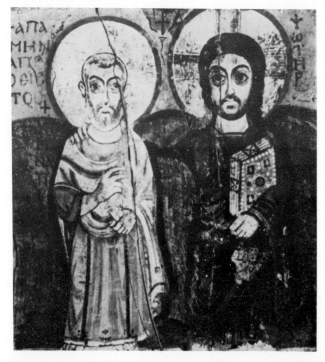

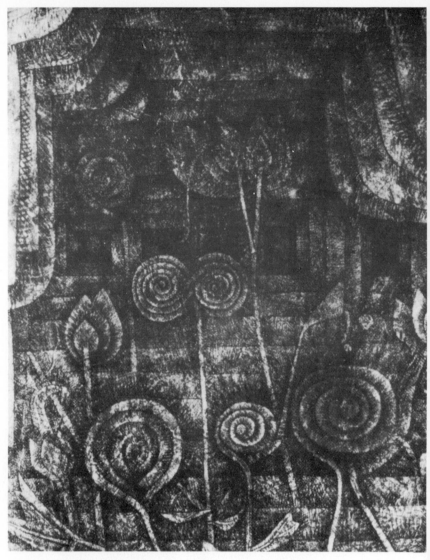

10. Spiral Blossoms, *Paul Klee*

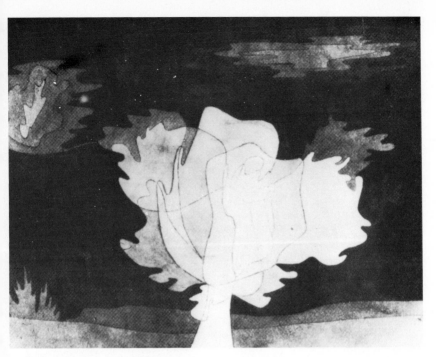

11. Before the Snow, *Paul Klee*

12. Demonry, *Paul Klee*

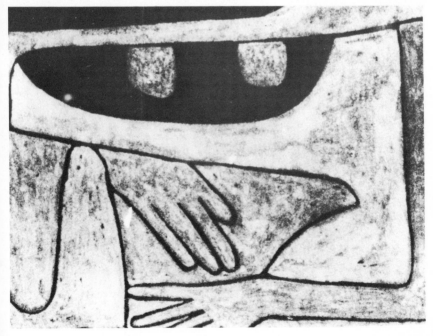

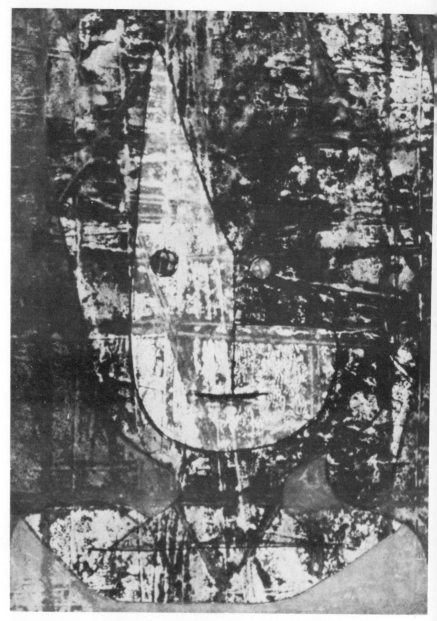

13. Saint Through a Window, *Paul Klee*

our intellects, then it would have been only right for God to have revealed himself as an intelligibly apprehensible abstraction.[39]

But what he did was to become man, and hence it is the painterly image which forms 'the most striking sign of the economy of God'.[40] In another perspective Theodore can be seen as applying to the struggle over the icons a specifically incarnational principle of theological reason. He insists that in the saving plan of God there can be no sharp distinction between the time of Jesus' earthly life and subsequent time. Just as Christ appeared to his disciples with all the attributes of humanity and was perceived to be divine *via* those attributes, so now he is discernible in the same way. Once the Word became flesh he did not subsequently become non-flesh, even to satisfy the implicit Iconoclast desire that the world be intelligible in its own terms again as before the disclosure of God in the form of Jesus' life. Patrick Henry, who sees this as the key to Theodore's thinking, has written that

It is a mistake to think that the Iconoclasts were rationalists and the Iconodules mystics. Both were determined to be rational. The whole question was what constituted rationality subsequent to an episode that was both the supreme revelation of God . . . and foolishness to the Greeks. The Iconoclastic Controversy brings into sharp focus the problem of the development of a distinctively christian mode of thinking. By disallowing the distinction between what could be said about the incarnation before the resurrection and what after, the Iconodules established a pattern of argument in which assertions about present conditions have direct and unavoidable implications for one's fundamental understanding of past conditions, since the past conditions, specifically that of the incarnation of the Son of God, are still in effect.[41]

In conclusion: if it is true that the heart of Iconophile theology lies in arguing a permanent alteration, through the incarnation, in what counts as rational in human thinking, then it is not perhaps surprising to find the high point of the Byzantine theology of the icon in a setting of *monastic* experience. The astonishing growth of monasticism from the fourth century onwards had been clear testimony to the deep and extensive feeling that the Christian ideal must have some more distinctive expression than in the empire. In 815 Theodore posed this question in just these terms of Church and state to the emperor's face.[42] For him, it has been said, the monastic church filled with brethren at prayer surrounded by the images of Christ, his mother and his saints, was the sign *par excellence* of the communion of saints, the place where men on earth should look for windows into heaven. To this radical opponent of the Imperial ideology the 'Christian empire', on the other hand, was 'only a fragment, one of the kingdoms of this world'.[43] Perhaps the best Christian art, like the best Christian politics, has an inescapably eschatological character, lying open to the future of God. This character is most palpable from within such an ambience of silence as monastic worship possesses. Pointing out that many of the greatest achievements of liturgical art, the plainsong of the Latin church, the iconography of Byzantine and Russian Orthodoxy, the buildings of the Romanesque and Gothic West, have been realized in or at any rate in close contact with monastic communities, A. M. Allchin suggests that only the recognition of a certain primacy of silence

> prevents us from falling into the fatal error of thinking that we have comprehended and can express the fulness of God's revelation whether in a closed system of human concepts or in purely human and worldly artistic techniques. . . . Like the monastic community, like the whole church, the work of an artist or a theologian (then) becomes an eschatological sign, a sign of the presence in this age of the indescribable glory of the age to come.[44]

CHAPTER SIX

The Shape of the Artwork

In considering the biblical foundations for the model of the artwork in christology, this essay has suggested that the form of divine revelation in Christ, witnessed by the renaissance of the metaphor of the artwork in the New Testament, itself opens up the way for a Christian iconography. An art might be created by the 'shaping and fashioning of visual images' which 'would add up to an exegesis of the events of revelation'. In so doing it would 'bring out a part, at least, of the meaning of the significant form of Christ' and thus throw light on the nature of revelation itself by offering us a model in which we may 'understand the revelatory disclosure'.[1] We have seen how, in its historical context, such an art emerged and found its legitimacy questioned but eventually vindicated by the Christian Church. It has several times been hinted that the iconographic achievement of the art of the ancient Church surpassed rather considerably the reflective understanding of art which those who lived by it and set out to theologize its significance themselves possessed. What we shall do in this chapter is to lay a groundwork for a contemporary theology of revelation in terms of the model of the artwork in which the aims of the exploration will be those set by Christian tradition, but the means – the materials – will be those of present-day art theory. As an historian of the patristic contribution to doctrine has written, 'True continuity with the age of the Fathers is to be sought not so much in the repetition of their doctrinal conclusions or even in the building upon them, but rather in the continuation of their doctrinal aims'.[2]

What is the artwork?

Artists are not dependent for their inspiration or their craft upon aestheticians, fortunately enough. Yet a sound grasp of the nature of distinctively artistic activity is no trivial thing. Firstly, false notions of what art is and where its significance lies may well hinder or prevent our receiving the disclosure which art-images make in its fullest scope. Secondly, any theological reflection on the way the artwork can be said to be revelatory – such as this essay will offer – must be as weak as the account of art on which it draws.

It is fortunate, therefore, that the resurgence of a visionary art with teaching to offer in the modern epoch has coincided with the rise of a school of aesthetics which takes artistic experience seriously as a unique form of communication not to be reduced to some more general category less than itself. This 'phenomenological' school works with the philosophical method of the same name whose keynote is the self-discipline of the knowing agent before the object. As Martin Heidegger, a pioneer of this method, wrote in his early *Being and Time*, the being in question must 'be seen as existing in its own self-disclosure'.[3] This re-direction of interest towards the object conceived in its own autonomy of existence is the more welcome in aesthetics since a rampant subjectivism has reigned there all too long.

If it be true that aesthetics as a distinct branch of philosophy is the creation of the eighteenth century, it is also true that the fascination of that century with the subject of taste has proved a *damnosa hereditas*.[4] It threatened to precipitate the understanding of the artwork into a morass of subjective individual feeling which tells us something about the accidents of history, nationality, culture, and temperament of the spectator but nothing about the artwork itself. Yet no aesthetic theory can be less satisfactory than one which places the grounds of judgement about art not in anything in the artwork itself but in pleasant or unpleasant sensations in us. On such a theory, to claim that a work has aesthetic merit is to say that you have certain feelings when you contemplate it or, alternatively, is to betray such feelings. For the rest we are handed over to the historian, the sociologist, and the psychologist for enlightenment about 'what in general are the causes of a feeling, why various societies produced and admired the works of art they did, why taste varies as it does within a given society and so forth'.[5] There are two immediate objections to this view. Firstly, it does not do justice to that minimum of experience which consists in enjoying, say, Botticelli's *Birth of Venus* in a distinctively aesthetic way. At the very least, we need to know what is the particular character of aesthetic pleasure, as distinct from pleasure of other sorts. Trying to account for going into rapture over the *Birth of Venus* by showing that this feeling falls under a general law relating wavy shapes, colour combinations, and human eyes makes such an ecstasy, as one English philosopher of art has said, 'excusable rather than intelligible'.[6] Secondly, the account of pleasure which underpins this aesthetic theory is rightly under fire in contemporary philosophical psychology. A sensation is usually locatable, but *A Midsummer Night's Dream* does not seem to give you pleasure in the eyes. If pleasure were a sensation then its connection with what it produced would be a causal one. It would only be as a result of induction that we could say on any given occasion what we were enjoying, as with the inferring of any causal link in the empirical realm.

> If, say, one had enjoyed listening to the first performance of a new overture, it would be a mere hypothesis that what one had enjoyed was listening to the overture and not, say, sitting in row G of the dress circle, This hypothesis would need to be verified in accordance with Mill's canons, one should listen to the overture again sitting in row F of the stalls and introspect carefully to see if the sensation occurred. This is clearly absurd. . . .[7]

What we enjoy in art is, rather, some aesthetically moving form. When we are looking at a Sisley landscape the object of our enjoyment is the painting itself, not the visual sensations. The pleasantness of the looking is logically prior to the pleasantness of the sensations. The feelings we have, when these are other than a joy of the mind in the form embodied sensuously in the canvas, are extrinsic and posterior to that enjoyment which makes the experience an experience of the beautiful.

I have now introduced a further but familiar concept, that of the *beautiful*. Familiar it may be, dangerous it certainly is, for the temptation is perennial to use the concept for some specifiable quality defined by a rule of artistic making like the celebrated 'Golden Number' in the science of proportion. All such definitions of the beautiful prove otiose because sooner or later they rule out of court artworks which speak powerfully to us while lacking the essential claimed for the beautiful. But this does not mean that the language of the beautiful should be abandoned. According to the phenomenological school, in calling a work of art beautiful we are doing two things. First, we are recommending it as an object which meets the criterion of any aesthetic object, the power to communicate with us through a configuration of matter. Mikel Dufrenne, the leading writer of this school, could hardly go further in freeing artists from an *a priori* concept of the *stylistically* beautiful when he declares that,

> The norm of the aesthetic object is invented afresh by each such object, and each has no other law than the one it makes for itself.[8]

Second, in calling the artwork beautiful we describe it by echoing a judgement made 'within' the artwork, rather than by us. Meaning is not projected on to an arrangement of paints or of masses of stone. It is already embodied and communicated there through its creator's handling of the sensuous. We can recognize beauty, therefore, without creating a theory of the beautiful. Indeed, there is no such theory to create. There is the stating of what aesthetic objects are, and to the degree that they are, they are beautiful.

This enables us to clear away one major misapprehension. The judgement that makes the aesthetic experience what it is should be distinguished from the judgements which express our special tastes by affirming our preferences. Taste is not the inner organization of aesthetic perception but merely something which sharpens or dulls it. We can acknowledge that a canvas is a work of art without appreciating it personally. We can, and perhaps more commonly do, appreciate an artwork without giving it properly aesthetic acknowledgement. For instance, you may be hugely appreciative of Holman Hunt's *The Light of the World*, but the appreciation may be directed to memories of childhood religiosity which it awakens. Our special preferences in art may dictate the breadth or narrowness of our vision, our errors and failures of appreciation. Their consequences may be enormous, as when neo-Classical observers failed to 'see' the English Gothic cathedrals. Hence the need to examine them and re-examine. It is in the moment that our aesthetic judgement ceases to specify such preferences and simply registers in the presence of the beautiful that it is wholly, universally valid and not simply valid 'for me'. This is so because at such a moment it lets the object speak and show itself for what it is. The historical conditioning of taste is no argument against aesthetic judgement of this kind. We need not fear that we are indulging in a piece of concealed solipsism when we describe an artwork, 'really' chatting away about ourselves. We are doing something mercifully more interesting than re-arranging our pleasurable sensations.

The artwork is rightly judged beautiful, or, otherwise expressed, itself, if it embodies the meaningful in the sensuous. The sensuous element is responsible for the artwork's peculiar plenitude and its uniquely imposing form of presence. It 'speaks to' us or 'strikes' us through the glory of the sensuous realm to which it belongs. R. G. Collingwood was mistaken in thinking that the primary reality of the artwork was an idea in the mind of the artist, only secondarily extruded more or less successfully into some material medium.[9] The 'weight' of the sensuous, rendered communicative by the artist's creative talent, accounts for the ability of the artwork to take an initiative with us and to be experienced by us as a kind of address. This sensory matrix necessarily remains an integral aspect of its being and its value to the perceiver. A modern Thomist, commenting on St Thomas' notion of the *splendor formae* in experiencing the beautiful rightly remarks that in the perception of beauty:

> the understanding, working through sensory intuition, is placed in the presence of a radiant intelligibility. . . . But this (act of presence), in as much as it bestows the joy of what is beautiful, cannot be disengaged or separated from its sensory matrix, and thus does not yield a *theoretical* knowledge of the sort expressible in a concept.[10]

The meaning embodied in the artwork is communicated, then, in a unique, *sui generis* manner. It is found in the very organization of the sensuous and lies in the spatial schemata of the canvas. This meaning defies translation into the clarity of prose, not because it is vacuous but because it is inexhaustible. Unlike other sorts of sign, the traffic-light, the flag of the nation, the linguistic signs of literal prose, we can set no limit to the plurality of readings that express the artwork. The multiple points of view spectators and critics find themselves taking up before a work of art, if they truly represent an effort to grasp its real character, testify to what Dufrenne would call

93

the 'depth' of the aesthetic object. No artwork can be taken in at a single glance. It must be lived with, and in the living will show us a multitude of faces, and an unlimited power to illuminate our experience.

As an embodiment of meaning in the sensuous order, the artwork communicates with us through two essential means. First of all, it is part of an *iconology*, a pattern of images and motifs in an artist's work or in a wider artistic tradition. A network of visual images forms in art a sign-system which is a kind of visual analogue to a language.[11] Just as a language provides the articulation for the basic set of perceptions available to the people who speak the language, so an iconology forms a possible world of aesthetic perceptions. Language in its rich metaphorical development takes up the literal sense of the world of natural objects and transforms the meanings we find ready made about us into a new world which is distinctively human. An artistic iconology likewise makes 'the world to which man belongs become the world which belongs to man'.[12] It depends on 'natural' meanings for the source of its forms, whether these are representational and figurative or abstract and formalistic. Just as a particular poet will rely on certain established metaphorical trans- formations of the literal in speech, so too an artist in his iconology will presuppose a background of stylistic convention from which his own creative innovation stands out. An iconology is always in debt to a particular cultural setting. At the same time, in the hands of a great artist, it has a power to communicate its new world of significance in a way which transcends that limited cultural setting from which it emerged.

We may take some examples of how an iconology works. We can begin with an art tradition touched in tracing the rise of a Christian theology of art, the art of the icon in the Eastern Church. That art has been described as 'a visual system conveying and giving support to the spiritual facts which underlie the whole liturgical drama'.[13] It is the distinctive feature of this art that it forms part of the wider iconology or sign system of the Christian liturgy itself. It seeks to express a structure of belief that can be seen most clearly in the fully developed form of the Byzantine church building which Father Gervase Mathew dated to the ninth century. 'Once a church was conceived as itself an image', he wrote, 'the relationship between religious art and architecture grew close to the point of fusion. Both gain their meaning from the liturgy and the form of presentation of mosaics became determined by the use to which they might be put by worshippers within the building.'[14] The iconographic scheme of the Byzantine church involves an iconology that discloses the 'shape' of the Christian universe of meaning. First, there is the divine world shown in the dome and on the high vaults; second, on the squinches or pendentives and upper parts of the walls are scenes devoted to the life of Christ, and thirdly on the lower or secondary vaults and the lower walls are images of the holy men and women who already have a part in the redeemed world. Thus we have an expression of the *kenosis*, the descent of the transcendent God, showing itself in the events of the life of the Incarnate Word and his mother (classically in the Twelve Feasts: the annunciation, the nativity, the presentation in the temple, the baptism, the transfiguration, the raising of Lazarus, the entry into Jerusalem, the crucifixion and the resurrection, the ascension, Pentecost and Mary's assumption). That eruption of God into the world of human forms is further embodied in the men and women who testify by the form of their lives to the reality of transfiguration by God's grace which is the goal of the incarnation. These images are portraits of a deified humanity, of men and women who have recovered the capacity to show forth the divine which had been obscured by sin, and who now share in the festival of the new heaven and new earth. The Kingdom of God, the heart of the Christian faith and hope, is evoked for men by this iconology. It can be apprehended by the worshippers because in the iconography and architecture of the building it is projected in visual terms into the space of the church. The iconology of the Eastern Church is not, we should notice, purely an affair of themes superimposed on the painterly techniques of artists to give art a theological coherence. It is partly achieved by the distinctively painterly means of colour and line. One line of the tradition of aesthetic interpretation in Russian Orthodoxy in modern times sees in icons 'Russia's mediaeval philosophy in colour'. The colour system, it is said, carries a 'theological interpretation of colour'.[15] Trubetskoy noted that gold, which is not strictly part of the spectrum, that is, not 'in creation', occupies a central place in the colour scale. He thought that in an artwork like Rublev's *Christ in Glory* in the Tretyakov all other colours are related to gold as the symbol of the uncreated, denoting divine energy and splendour. In the Rublev Christ the robes of the figure shimmer with a gold web of the finest lines called *assist*, and delicate shafts of golden light irradiate from the centre to the corners of the icon. It is possible, then, to see in this technique the painterly expression of the communication of grace.

The rich iconology of *Marc Chagall* would repay close attention for in it we can see a variety of disparate materials – the imagery of Old Testament and Hassidic Judaism and to some extent the New Testament, memories of childhood in Vitebsk and the searing public events of two world wars in Europe, a stylistic vocabulary drawn from the post-Impressionist tradition of late nineteenth century Europe and from the art of the Russian icon – all pressed into the service of creating an artistic 'world' which is different from any of the 'worlds' of its sources. It is a world which attempts to hold them together and to heal them, for its iconography everywhere expresses a desire and pursuit of the whole. The conviction that the blessing of wholeness is available shows itself in Chagall's work in the simultaneous appearance of images of destruction, crucifixion, and holocaust with images of pure lyrical loveliness – flowers, animals, musical instruments. The meanings Chagall creates are fully seen only when his various images and canvases are related to each other. So, for instance, in the wedding scene in his *Life* we know from other contexts that the elongated rising sweep of the figures is linked with resurrection. In *The Green Horse* there is an extraordinary density of meanings of the feminine, gathered together from images Chagall explored singly in other works. Here the woman is at once naked Aphrodite, loyal wife, protective Madonna.[16] Such iconology opens up that Chagallian world where God gives man his fulfilment in a glorious wholeness.

As a final example we may glance at the work of *Paul Klee*. Werner Haftmann in his study of Klee has brought out the variety of sources for Klee's treasury of forms: his discovery of an undreamt wealth of natural forms through his visits to Dohrn's great aquarium in Naples as a young man, and the artistic vocabulary he found in the tradition, above all that school of 'international Gothic' of central and northern Italy, culminating in the work of Gentile da Fabriano and Pisanello, in which Klee saw 'minuteness and precision in the service of a spiritual vision'.[17] Klee's creative energy was devoted to the task of bringing these formal resources into an iconology which would integrate them and raise them to a new power of artistic expressiveness. Haftmann has written that Klee

> found himself thinking, very much like Kleist, that the two bright peaks of knowledge are those of animals and of Gods, the one a paradisiac unawareness, the other the purest awareness of divinity. Between them, in a dark valley, stands man, longing to attain to both of these peaks within himself, to achieve harmony, to discover the circle of the whole, to see, as Kleist says, 'whether perhaps the back door of paradise is open again'.[18]

In *Spiral Blossoms*, for example, the swell and curl of blossom provide a metaphor for the secret of life itself, combining botanical exactness with a sense of the miracle of organic growth. The sacramental power that Klee saw invested in the death and resurrection of nature in paintings like *Before the Snow* and *Arctic Thaw* led him to realize the early Romantic idea of an *Erdlebenbildkunst*, a pictorial art of the Life of the Earth, a series of visual metaphors in which, Klee said, he would make 'a cosmos of forms which is so similar to the Creation that only the slightest breath is needed to transform religious feeling, religion into fact'.[19] His mature iconology gives us a disclosure of the world as a unitary complex, embracing man and nature. The precise filigree of natural forms is brought together with a flowing line capable of expressing human feeling and creativity. 'Creation', he wrote, 'exists as genesis beneath the visible surface of a work.' He bequeathed us some highly instructive accounts of this process whereby a picture turns out to be 'a crystallisation of things experienced, things which have grown, things which have been made and things which are known'. Yet there is little here to prepare us for the disruption in his work that generated a fresh iconology under the stress of the political events of the late 1930s, signalling as they did a coming world conflagration. The outlines of his forms suddenly acquire a rounded, taut, bursting quality; they become the signs of a world bloated with excess, an unwholesome repletion that masks corruption and decomposition as in his *Monsters in Readiness* and *Demonry*. At the same time a whole hierarchy of angels enters his canvases with *Archangel*, *Angelus Militans* and *Angel Overflowing*: in relation to the slime of the images of decadence these bear the meaning, in this new iconological pattern, of vehicles of transcendence. They are creatures who refuse to belong to an old world sunk in a corrupt finitude. Klee's final pictures, *Glass Façade*, say, or *Saint out of a Window*, are festive images with a distantly radiant use of colour, variations, it has been said, on the theme of a being whose earthly light is going out, but who is nevertheless irradiated from a source in some other world.[20]

The second means whereby the artwork communicates with us is this. The world of meaning constituted by the iconology of the painting is always a world shot through with a singular affective quality. This quality of feeling is what makes the world of the artwork as we would say 'expressive' to us. In looking at a picture we should be first of all disinterested. To allow the artwork to speak we must not muffle it by a barrage of our own prior feelings, memories and mental habits. When on achieving this suspension of egoism we succeed in seeing the artwork in the pregnant aesthetic sense of 'to see' we find that the feeling-quality of disinterestedness gives way to fresh and original feelings called forth by the artwork itself. These feelings lead on in good art appreciation to a type of reflection which is sympathetic, rather than objectifying. Feelings do not become irrelevant to seeing, as when we have a thing taped and are content to let it be 'out there'. On the contrary, the role of reflection, in the best art-criticism whether our own made to ourselves or other people's offered in print, is to clarify and support the feelings we have before the artwork. A response of this kind is not emotional in the sense of vapid and vacuous. It is a precise, appropriate response because it is a right reading of the 'singular affective quality' which characterizes the canvas before our eyes. Our feeling-response to the contours, colours, and painterly technique of Van Gogh's canvases, for example, *is* our reading of the tragic world he portrays in his paintings. Dufrenne goes so far as to call such feeling a kind of knowledge rather than a kind of emotion.[21] By means of it the painting reveals a world to us, an experience comparable to the 'Got it!' of knowing. Emotion, on the other hand, is merely a reaction to a world already given.

The artwork, therefore, has a revelatory power. We have already noted in looking at St Nicephorus' theology of the icon that the image is, at its heart, an intentional reality. It is a 'being towards', a sign. It is this capacity of the image to point beyond itself while remaining the absolutely necessary and wonderful medium of what it signifies that we refer to when we speak of its 'revelatory' capacity. The artwork is essentially part of the real in which we are interested. It never becomes superfluous. Yet at the same time our attention is drawn to it not for its own sake but for the content it embodies. It is never surpassed as a medium of the peculiar knowledge it leads to, but it is in its nature to lure us on, away from itself. A Russian Orthodox commentator on the art of the icon wrote of that explicitly theological art something which is true in an extended sense of all art:

> The icon is a visible sign of the splendour of invisible presence. The space granted us when we follow the cue of the icon in no sense imprisons anything. Rather, it shares in a presence and is hallowed by it. The icon has no existence of its own. It simply guides us to what really is.[22]

Indirectly, but no less genuinely, the artwork also reveals its creator. Except by accident it does not of course offer us information about the artist, the kind of data that the historian gathers. It does something more. It places us in communion with him, ushering us into a presence which the historian could not hope to communicate. The biography of an artist can only tell us about a man precisely as artist if it has first been instructed by his art. The artwork speaks of its creator by what is called *style*, that is:

> a certain procedure which is recognised by the stylisation it produces, . . . by the substitution of forms intended by the spirit for the inchoate proliferation of forms in nature.[23]

An acanthus leaf, a Vermeer interior, an Annunciation of the Macedonian school, each betrays a pattern, *un dessin*, answering to a plan, *un dessein* in Dufrenne's skilful pun. To attain a style is 'to do what we want to do'. Whenever a particular way of treating matter, or arranging colour, line, and mass, can be seen as enabling some vision of things there we have style and there the artist himself appears in his work.

The artwork as the shaper of existence

To hold that there is a genuine issue of knowing from aesthetic experience is not to deny that looking at a painting is a different sort of cognitive experience from reading about painting, or devouring a theological treatise. There is no detachable conclusion in the experience of a work of art which can be acquired and used apart from the work itself. The yield of the experience is not an instrument, a fact or a truth. But the experience of the artwork is not for that reason a nugatory one. It can be powerful enough to alter the meaning and weight of all the rest of my experience, before and after it.[24] Art requires and releases an *askesis* or discipline of vision so that we learn how to look with a purity of insight into the heart of human life.[25] Such looking shifts our whole way of reading the significance of the world. In its wake we find our own existence reshaped from the experience of what we have seen. A philosopher who regards art as quite central in the task of charting the various modalities of human understanding, Hans-Georg Gadamer, put the matter as follows:

> The power of the artwork suddenly takes the person experiencing it out of the context of his life, and yet relates him back to the whole of his existence. In the experience of art there is present a fulness of meaning which belongs not only to this particular content or object but stands rather for the meaningful whole of life. An aesthetic experience always contains the experience of an infinite whole. Precisely because it does not combine with others to make one open experiential flow, but immediately represents the whole, its significance is infinite.[26]

Perhaps it takes a philosopher of art who is herself a writer of imaginative fiction to show how such experience actually shapes the lives of human beings. In her novel *The Bell* Iris Murdoch narrates a visit by Dora to the National Gallery in London. In earlier sections of the novel the moral and emotional challenge of Dora's world has been transformed into the stuff of fantasy by her 'destructive, trance-like solipsism'. But that is quite set aside by a moment in the art gallery. The artworks before her bestow on her a sense of reality beyond herself, and the experience is spoken of in terms of revelation. The paintings 'spoke to her kindly, yet in sovereign tones' and Dora

> felt that she had had a revelation. She looked at the radiant, sombre, powerful canvas of Gainsborough and felt a sudden desire to go down on her knees before it, embracing it, shedding tears. . . . She gave a last look at the paintings, still smiling, as one might smile in a temple, favoured, encouraged and loved.[27]

Rather earlier, it has occurred to Dora that perhaps here at last was 'something real and something perfect'. She wonders 'who had said that, about perfection and reality being in the same place?' *The Bell* was written in 1958, six years before the appearance of Miss Murdoch's essay 'The Idea of Perfection' so the answer to Dora's question is probably 'Plato' rather than the consciously ironic one of 'Miss Murdoch herself'. The idea is a leading one, however, in her own philosophy.

She defines 'reality' as that which is revealed in particular moral situations to the patient eye of love.

> As moral agents, we have to try and see justly, to overcome prejudice, to avoid temptation, to control and curb imagination, to direct reflection.[28]

Morally we always act in the light of an idea of perfection by which we come to see that A, which superficially resembles B, is really better than B. This we do without our having the sovereign idea of perfection within our conceptual grasp. Beyond the present limits of our moral vision lies the authority of the good, necessary to us because

> the realism required for goodness is a kind of intellectual ability to perceive what is true, which is automatically at the same time a suppression of self.[29]

For this reason, art and morals are 'two aspects of a single struggle'. Through the canvases of Velasquez or Titian, she says, we discover something about the real quality of human nature as it is envisaged in the artist's own just and compassionate vision. The appreciation of art is

> a completely adequate entry into (and not just analogy of) the good life, since it is the checking of selfishness in the interest of seeing the real.[30]

The artwork is a 'sacrament of good energy', activating our latent power to existence as men and women of clear vision who live by reverence for the real. It 'inspires love in the highest part of the soul' by its perfection of form, for this at once invites an unpossessive contemplation and at the same time resists absorption into the selfish dream-life of the consciousness. 'We surrender ourselves to its authority with a love which is unpossessive and unselfish.'[31]

That Miss Murdoch's suggestions here are not merely a critical prop for a concern of her own novels will become evident from turning, in conclusion, to a novelist of a very different stamp, D. H. Lawrence.[32] Lawrence had seen Fra Angelico's *The Last Judgement* in St Mark's Dominican priory in Florence. It appears in his novel *The Rainbow* where, in a phrase of Lawrence's own in *Phoenix*, Anna and Ursula Brangwen 'dwell' in the painting and come to find in it a visual revelation of their destiny. The theme of *The Rainbow* is the striving of men and women for consummation in love. According to Lawrence this theme pervades the Western artistic tradition. 'Dürer, Fra Angelico, Botticelli, all sing of the moment of consummation, some of them still marvelling and lost in wonder at the other being'.[33] He used *The Last Judgement* for some of his imagery in *The Rainbow*, part of the thread from which the imaginative existence of his characters is spun, and he made the painting actually appear within the narrative itself as a reality affecting that existence within the fictional space of the book. The iconography of *The Last Judgement* represents the opposites of salvation and damnation, heaven and hell. Lawrence portrays these polarities in his novel by contrasting illumination and darkness, inclusion and exclusion, consummation and annihilation. After the quarrel over Will's beloved carving of the creation of Eve, Anna tearfully confesses to her parents that Will's coldness has prevented her from announcing that she is pregnant. Here and in the reconciliation that follows, Lawrence draws on the visual elements of the Fra Angelico canvas:

the 'little circle' of characters, Will's 'entry' when he appears illuminated 'through the open door (as) the level rays of sunset poured
in, shining on the floor', and their walking home hand in hand
while 'the blaze of light in her heart was too beautiful and dazzling'.
Later, Anna finds among Will's reproductions a print of the *Entry
of the Blessed into Paradise*, the side of *The Last Judgement* that
portrays man's salvation. The painting

> filled Anna with bliss. The beautiful, innocent way in which the
> Blessed held each other by the hand as they moved towards the
> radiance, the real, real, angelic melody, made her weep with
> happiness. The floweriness, the beams of light, the linking of
> hands, was almost too much for her, too innocent. Day after day
> she came shining through the door of Paradise, day after day she
> entered into the brightness. The child in her shone till she herself
> was a beam of sunshine. . . . How happy she was, how gorgeous
> it was to live; to have known . . . a terrible purifying fire, through
> which she had passed for once to come to this peace of golden
> radiance, when she was with child and innocent and in love with
> her husband and with all the many angels hand in hand.[34]

The painting creates in Anna a yearning for 'a fulness of peace and
blessedness'. It also enables her to recognize the sense of creation
that 'shines' within her, and gives her an experience of the transcendent harmony of the Angels.

A painting, therefore, may serve as a profoundly educative lure
for man. Indeed, in the highly visual culture of medieval Russia the
very word for education, *obrazovanie*, suggests 'becoming like the
forms', the images.[35] In this there is a certain priority granted to
the artwork over the conscious effort of the perceiver to grasp the
vision it holds out. It is far from being merely an occasion for
rehearsing something already known but in need of more vivid
illustration.

> Inasmuch as it is a structure it has, so to speak, found its measure
> in itself and measures itself by nothing outside it. . . . It no longer
> permits of any comparison with reality as the secret measure of
> all copied similarity. It is raised above all such comparisons
> . . . because a superior truth speaks from it. . . . The world of the

103

work of art, in which play expresses itself fully in the unity of its course, is in fact a wholly transformed world. By means of it everyone recognises that that is how things are. . . .[36]

. . . .the picture is an ontological event and hence cannot be properly understood as the object of aesthetic consciousness. Rather, it is to be grasped in its own ontological structure . . . (for) in it being becomes meaningfully visible.[37]

CHAPTER SEVEN

The Artwork and Christian Revelation

We now have in our possession a grasp of some of the aspects of the artwork and its significance in human life: the next stage in this essay must be to draw on these in order to suggest lines of thought for a renewed theology of revelation on the model of the artwork. A teaching of this kind, drawing on the metaphor of the image in the Scriptures and the experience of art in Christian life and worship, has been, we have noted, of major importance in the theological articulation of the Christian faith in the tradition. What is more, its emergence – like the rise of church art itself – was no accident, no matter of mere historical contingency. It was, I have argued, an apt, reasonable, and predictable comment on the form in which the distinctive meaning of Christianity was first given, and as such that theology of the image provides one of the richest veins of ore in exploring what Christians mean by 'revelation'.

The theology of revelation as a distinct subject in its own right is a fairly modern invention. Ever since Kant's monumental study of the varieties and limits of human knowledge, Christian theologians had perforce to consider more fully and explicitly than before the claims of the distinctively Christian knowledge of God to be a genuine, veridical way of knowing. What indications are there in the constitution of the human subject that might lead us to think of man as able to recognize and assimilate a divine disclosure of the nature of reality and the role and meaning of man's existence? How shall we speak about the cognitive side of God's self-communication to us in the experience of the Christian life, of salvation, worship and prayer? What analogies will help to display its character and intelligibility? Sometimes, indeed, the impression has been given in modern theology that exploration of the tradition of meaning in the Christian Church's life and the relating of that tradition to secular experience may not begin at all until we have put down our pens

105

at the close of a treatise on revelation. That would be absurd – and is rightly stigmatized by one historian of the theology of revelation as an 'inflation' of the subject, the bitter fruit of the 'hypertrophy of the epistemological problem after Kant'.[1] Salvation in itself, God's gracious healing and exaltation of humanity to share in his own life, is no more a way of thinking and knowing than is love or lexicography. Yet as soon as we enquire into the way we become aware of any of these distinctive contents in our human experience we find ourselves confronted with epistemology, with the bewildering variety of distinctive modalities of understanding and styles of intellectual procedure which our commerce with the variety of reality requires. The New Testament witnesses to the awareness, on the part of the first Christian generation, that the experience of the Christian realities presupposes a divine communication of truth and a divinely enabled way of knowing on the part of man. As a recent christologian has put it, even if words explicitly designed to carry a concept of revelation are relatively few in the New Testament, the belief that God can and does make himself known to man is quite fundamental to the literature.[2]

It would be impossible in a brief essay such as this to relate systematically the aesthetic theology of revelation I am proposing to even the more important and influential of the classical theologies of revelation in the history of Christian thought. It would also, perhaps, be doubtfully useful. At any rate, the use of any such proceeding would consist in placing a theology of 'the art of God incarnate' in terms of the tasks and services that other accounts of revelation have been able to perform. Books of theology are of value if they prove capable of shedding a little fresh light on the Christian data which they presuppose; often, those data are most clearly seen in the course of collaboration, or tension or even conflict between diverse theological ways of speaking of God. As Father Edward Schillebeeckx, O. P., has written,

> Although supernatural truth, like every truth, is absolute and unchangeable, it still shares, insofar as it is known by us in faith, in human imperfection and thus in the evolutive character of every human possession of truth. Even though every such possession of truth is adequately true (that is, it is not simultaneously true and not-true), this adequately true possession is not exhaus-

tive. Every insight is therefore capable of growth and amplification. Every theological system is therefore essentially imperfect, incomplete, capable of further inner growth, and in need of amplification from other systems.[3]

We may hope, therefore, to find in the theologies of the past and present in all their rich complementarity, a challenge for the sketch about to be presented. Will a theology of the image be able to integrate and display the achievements of these theologies in the elucidation of Christian faith? Will it be able, in so doing, to illuminate the data of the theology of revelation in a freshly significant way? I shall argue that the approach to revelation suggested here does have a remarkable interpretative power for those aspects of the subject which now one, now another theology have brought to light.

And yet there are two caveats to be entered here as precautions against theological hubris. First, the very idea of a theological model entails some realistic limits to the theologian's sense of the gain one single range of comparison – however illuminating – can bring to faith. A rich plurality of models should be his aim, and it is one that is fully compatible with serious attention to the need for establishing coherence and hierarchy between the models he uses. Second, the impulse to form an integrated and over-arching system in any realm of enquiry, the 'blessed rage for order', good and necessary as it is, must be checked by the realization that (to continue Schillebeeckx's words)

a system is not concerned with the system itself, but with reality. In itself the system has no value: to affirm that it did would be tantamount to making the system, to making theology itself, the object of theology, instead of the mystery of salvation.[4]

To draw some aspect of God's actual self-disclosure out of shadow by some slight infusion of light is more worthwhile, therefore, than the flooding of the history of theologies of revelation with a tropical sun.

It is probably fair to say that four approaches or mentalities have been paramount in theologies of revelation. Firstly, it is possible to understand the revelatory disclosure in terms of historical event or historical fact. Faith in the revealing God, on this view, is primarily faith in the God who acts, transforming the historical process by his interventions; and these events – above all, those that make up the history of Israel and the story of Jesus – registered, remembered, narrated, and celebrated, disclose the direction of God's purposes in history and thereby enable us to know the character of the God who is history's Lord. The original revelatory acts of God (the 'public constitutive revelation') are brought within the scope of our minds by the word of Scripture and the word of preaching in the life of the Church (the 'explicative and continuing phase of revelation'). This approach has the merit of situating revelation in the context of the openness of human history to God and of stressing its character as a dimension of public experience, open in principle to investigation and scrutiny. But inquiry into the events which carry revelatory value at once indicates that these events need not be interpreted as carrying the weight of significance the Christians attach to them. Revelation cannot possibly be mere fact, in the sense of a verifiable historical occurrence. It is fact pregnant with an abiding divine significance which must somehow be 'read'.[5]

This brings us to the second dominant motif in the theology of revelation: revelation as a corpus of doctrine. Here the model being applied is not that of positive history – although the approach is, in point of fact, quite heavily dependent on a capacity to recover historical situations where the *ipsissima verba* of Moses' speech with Yahweh and Israel, or those of Jesus, were delivered. The implicit model in this kind of theology is that of the teacher with his disciple. Revelation is conceptual – it is the communication and appropriation of eternal truths, mediated by oral or written instruction. The strength of this 'enlightenment' model lies in its concern with the intelligibility and authority of revelation. Its weaknesses are at least two-fold. First, as I have suggested, insofar as it rests on the claim to plot an unbroken chain of testimony, giving access to the precise words of the central teaching figure in the original experience of revelation, it is vulnerable in the same manner as the pure historical model. Second, if we could manage to separate off from apostolic comment 'a body of Christ's sayings which by themselves surely and sufficiently determine saving truth',[6] it is highly unlikely that we could draw out from the gospel tradition anything like a coherent scheme of propositions. 'I have heard it wisely said', remarked the late Austin Farrer, 'that in Scripture there is not a line of theology and of philosophy not so much as an echo'.[7] The proponents of the teaching model may then reasonably respond by re-structuring their model as a matter less of propositions than of metaphors. Great verbal images, it is said, are, in any case, the only possible vectors of a revelation in language: the merely literal would collapse beneath the weight of carrying some ultimate significance for human existence such as revelation posits. To follow Farrer, 'These tremendous images . . . set forth the supernatural mystery which is the heart of the teaching. Without them the teaching would not be supernatural revelation, but instruction in piety and morals. It is because the spiritual instruction is related to the great images, that it becomes revealed truth'.[8] The original subjective appropriation of revelation, on this view, lies in the germination of image-seeds which Christ had sown in the minds of the apostolic generation. It would be wrong to suppose that such an approach necessarily launches us on a sea of subjectivism and arbitrary interpretation of the gospel tradition. Farrer's study of the images of the Trinity in the New Testament is instructive. As he sums up his projected method,

> When we have isolated the image of the Trinity, and studied it in itself, we can then proceed to ask what place it occupies in the world of New Testament images – whether dominant or subordinate, vital or inessential: and how other images are affected by it. After that we can, if we like, go on to ask what metaphysical comment the New Testament image of the Trinity provokes, and which subsequent theological conceptualisations do least violence to it.[9]

Yet as this writer himself admits, the images without the events would remain shadows on the clouds. The 'great images' interpreted the events of Christ's ministry, death, and resurrection: there must be an interplay between event and image, and how is that to be described? How is the total situation of revelation to be envisaged if we are to close that rupture which looks so alarmingly like the gap between fact and interpretation that yawned out at us from the model of pure history?

It is here that a third approach to the theology of revelation in the history of theology may be expected to help: it may be hallmarked the mystical motif, for it stresses that revelation is a strictly ineffable encounter with God in act, in which the metaphors of 'prophetic knowledge'[10] or the symbols of the Liturgy in a 'theology of the Mysteries'[11] serve to evoke or induce the original revelatory experience as well as the subsequent experience of faith that flows from that. This type of revelation theology stresses that the revelatory event has, most importantly, a subjective pole. It occurs within man, in addition to its foundation of signs and triggers in the world outside him. Very often this model of mystical encounter includes an attempt to spell out features of the human subject that show his openness to transcendence, and this is vital to the model if it is not to lead the theologican into an espousal of sheer irrationality. Because the human spirit moves constantly in a search for the fulfilment of its capacity to take in being, having a kind of infinitude in its own powers of knowing and loving, we can say that there is an in-built possibility that man may recognize the signs of such a transcendent fulfilment if it were disclosed to him.[12] The role of metaphor and liturgical symbol in this comes about because man's ordering to the self-revealing God is not a power to apprehend God directly as an object before him. Man's knowledge of God is itself 'transcendental', in the word commended by the Jesuit metaphysician of mystical experience Père Joseph Maréchal: it is based on knowledge of God as of a higher order, implicit in particular experience and postulated by it.[13] The major defect of this model, as Hans Urs von Balthasar has pointed out[14] lies in its tendency to permit the collapse of the distinctively Christian truth-claims into claims about simple exemplary illustrations of our understanding of the human spirit in its relation to God. For how may we bring out the distinctiveness, much less the uniqueness, of revelation in Christ – the centre-point of the Christian experience of privileged revelation-bearing moments in human history – if by 'revelation' we mean only the provision of mystical encounters in which man's 'nisus' or drive towards transcendence is released and fulfilled? Bound up with this criticism is a second, that the given historical appearance and reality of Jesus Christ seem to be simply an 'occasion' for revelation on this view, rather than its very form. But this would be to secure immunity against the disadvantages of the 'pure history' and 'enlightenment' models at the enormous cost of serious interest in the historically embedded and historically displayed in the Christian religion.

That centrality of Christ in the theology of revelation (and behind that the importance of those other historical moments in the history of Israel that yield the sense of God which Jesus pre-supposed in speaking to his contemporaries of his 'Father') might be restored if we nudged the mystical model out of our focus and replaced it with a model of 'meeting between persons', the 'I-Thou' model for encounter with God which was brought into prominence by Martin Buber and subsequently given Christian application. Father Piet Schoonenberg has insisted that the 'openness' of the human spirit to transcendence is not only a matter of the more than finite capacity of human powers of knowing and loving: it is also a question of the social character of his being.

> One of the most eloquent expressions of it [he writes] is to be found in the fact that the human child must still learn all the patterns of movement with which the young animal is equipped from birth. Thus man shows himself as a nature most profoundly defined by its openness – for the gift of others. The dialectics of a natural longing for an unmerited gift, of a desire for what can only be gift and be desired as gift is proper to man; it almost forms his definition.[15]

On this view, the apprehension of the transcendent in revelation, if it is genuinely to be, and to be recognized as, man's fulfilment can only be an affair of a meeting with another personal reality, God as one who bestows himself freely in order to establish a communion of life with the human person. The particular experiences which serve as signs of this inter-subjective meeting do not give us an understanding of God or of ourselves in relation to God, strictly speaking; rather, they precipitate us into actual relationship. The Yahweh of the Old Testament, the Son of the New, are not so much known about as simply encountered in a meeting which has all the indefinability of falling in love. Here the primacy and initiative of the God who comes to meet man in the personal relationship of covenant, Old and New, is safeguarded surely enough, but it may still be questioned whether this personalist model can do justice to the form of the historical appearing of this personal appeal to

111

man. It has no way of speaking, for instance, of the relation between the Jesus of history and the Christ of the Church's Easter faith – yet establishing the continuity and integrity of these two 'forms' of revelatory occasion is vital to the historicity of Christian revelation. It is, further, rather unclear that there can be such a self-unveiling of the person as the model indicates without a medium of 'knowing about' in which that disclosure can take place and a precipitate of 'knowledge about' to which it leads.

This brief survey of the varieties of revelation-theology offers us some kind of agenda for the subject. It seems that we need to be able to articulate the character of revelation in terms of an interplay of fact and significance, or of event and interpretation. Second, we need to show how through the mediation of signals or signs in this interplay the human capacity for self-transcendence towards the divine is realized. Third, a satisfactory account must show how man is led thereby to an awareness of the ultimately personal values in existence as these might be manifested in fully concrete historical reality, in a quite specific form of life. In such a revelatory form, the evidence for the light of revelation would be open to our perception without our 'subjecting that light to the standards and laws of those perceiving it'.[16]

It is remarkable that a number of the features of the artwork that we have considered in the last chapter, and, obliquely, throughout this essay, seem to stand out as a pattern reflecting this constellation of demands in the search for a model in the theology of revelation. Firstly, in the artwork the configured materials of the object as it leaves the artist's hands are certainly fact, yet the artwork is only constitutive of the aesthetic experience when the perceiver approaches it with that sympathy which allows him to 'read' its affective world. Similarly, an adequate account of revelation must show the grounding of revelation in the historical – and therefore embodied and sensuous – order, where an event may strike us as expressing the divine 'speaking' to us through the peculiar plenitude of some experience. The 'disinterested' looking in which a man temporarily suspends the systematically interpretative function of his own presuppositions and convictions, tastes, and interests in order to let the artwork stand forth in its own integrity releases, through the affective intensity of the inner 'world' of the artwork, a new set of feelings. Through this experience he comes to inhabit

112

that world of meaning it carries, by means of a communion of sympathy. Likewise, before the event which is the given, historical foundation of the revelatory event as an encounter between God and man, not just any kind of scrutiny is apt to let the event yield its full significance. It requires a suspension of the screening process by which we determine what is or is not possible within the imaginative borders of reality we occupy, what is or is not compatible with God or man as we have theorized them. Not less important, the 'disinterested' perceiver must lay aside the tendency to exploit events in terms of his own fears and åspirations, for these will project on to them a character not their own. Once this discipline has been achieved, he may find that the event in question discloses to him an unsuspectedly rich source of meaning, a whole new world into which he is attracted by the weight of evident truth and goodness it bears.

The revelatory event breaks in on a man, as the aesthetic experience arises in a moment of communion from the art object in gallery or church, and he finds himself reorganizing his own world of meaning, what counts for him as 'the real', in its light. In the course of that, just as the artwork can shape an existence, moving us to the suppression of self so that fidelity to ultimate values may replace the distortions of the relentless ego, so the revelatory event proves able to place us in touch with an absolutely satisfying and complete hold on the reality that blesses us with its own truth, even if it calls on us for a painful reshaping of our lives. The revelatory event satisfies our nisus towards transcendence by disclosing to us the inexhaustibly satisfying reality we call 'God' drawing near to meet us.

This it does, secondly, through the mediation of signs. Just as the artwork communicates its full meaning only in the context of iconology, an interrelating set of images, so the reciprocities and echoes between events that we may suspect to be revelatory in force – their *typological* connections – are what give us the full meaning of the revelatory event, which is never to be looked at in isolation, as a lone image uncontextualized in its iconology. As G. W. H. Lampe has said of the Old Testament, 'It is the pattern of divine action which the prophet discerns, rather than the recurrence of the outward historical events; but for him, as for Israelite thought as a whole, divine action is mediated in the actual events of history.'[17]

113

This recapitulation of the rhythm of divine action evident in the history of the past involves a pattern established out of a variety of events and occasions, as the setting forth of the significance of the mission, death, and resurrection of Jesus in terms of a number of strands of Old Testament revelatory occasions amply shows.

This 'iconology', however, is not simply a way of getting objective history into a pleasing arrangement. It has designs on us, corresponding to our third demand. It communicates a personal meaning which requires a personal response. We are not meant to see the image-system of Chagall, for instance, as a mere ordering of his various artistic perceptions of the world, but as a call on us to review our sense of the possibilities of existence which his personal vision of wholeness lights up. Such an iconology, by its own supremely challenging statement of human values, requires us to review the whole range of perceptions of meaning we have previously found. In this way the artwork calls us to personal self-scrutiny, crisis, and growth in a unique form of personal encounter. As A. C. Charity has written of biblical typology:

> It is concerned much less, more or less speculatively, with the past and future states of man and God, than with the neglected demand which the divine acts imply, that man become what they make him able to be, an analogical counterpart to the analogical actions of God, a representative of God and his action to others; and thus typology . . . focuses or 'applies' past and future in the present 'word' of them, and exhorts each present age to repentance.[18]

Charity's account concludes by referring to revelation as word: what place does the theology of revelation on the model of the artwork have for the whole linguistic dimension of Christianity, and – above all, of course – for the scriptural witness?

It is where the model seems most weak that it may well have hidden resources to illuminate the subject. One of the most difficult and controverted problems in speaking of the coherence of New Testament revelation or the 'unity' of the Church's own Scriptures lies in the diversity of New Testament theologies as to the significance of the saving events they presuppose. Firstly, these theologies *are* notably diverse – as was clear in the patristic period

114

for, say, Paul and John and has since become clearer for the rest of the New Testament, and especially the Synoptic Gospels, with the rise of redaction criticism. Secondly, if we attempt to remove their original contributions in an attempt to recover the voice of the historical Jesus the operation proves not to be impossible or worthless (as for instance, the work of the great German exegete Joachim Jeremias shows) but in terms of the world of meaning the New Testament can show us, it does leave us with a meagre account of the novelty of revelation in Christ. May it be suggested that these various New Testament theologies are aptly compared to what I have spoken of above as 'the best art-criticism', that which 'clarifies and supports the feelings the perceiver experiences before the artwork'?[19] The work of Matthew or John or the author of the Letter to the Hebrews may be conceived as a reading of the significance of the form of Jesus Christ, a reading which, as their reception into the Canon shows, was accepted as enabled by a genuine communion of sympathy and disinterested receptiveness before the image of God in Christ. The variety of the readings is far from being an objection to the revelatory value of the life, death, and vindication of Jesus since, as we have said, the multiple points of view of worthy critics represent an effort to grasp the very nature of the object and in so doing 'their convergence testifies to . . . its "depth"'.[20]

How may the model of the artwork satisfy those demands for a sound theology of revelation that are made by the model of personal encounter? Surely by provoking us to see in the figure of Christ disclosure of his personal source, 'the Father', analogous to the style's disclosure of the artist in the artwork. The characteristic qualities of Jesus' acting and response to others, especially that abiding and unmistakable feature of self-emptying obedience from love and unto death which marks his activity, forms the style of the artwork of Christ. We do not look for the Father behind this style, as though it were a mere material integument which had to be laid aside: this style simply is the disclosure of the artist, the Father of Christ. 'He who has seen me, has seen the Father; how can you say, "Show us the Father?"'[21] In the world opened up to us by Christ, therefore, we are established in a unique personal communion with the Father, before a presence and countenance that no other materials could yield us.

Finally, this personal encounter is mediated in a quite specific,

115

concrete, and particular form of life, that of Jesus Christ. We shall
turn in a moment to consider the christological possibilities of the
model of the artwork. Here it will perhaps suffice to say that the
combination of sharpened sense of particularity and deepened sense
of the mystery of being that the artwork gives us should enable us
to place satisfactorily the respective roles of cataphatic or affirmative
knowing and apophatic or negative knowing in the knowledge
proper to awareness of the self-revealing God. Natural theology
does not offer an epistemology that can do justice to this mystery.
Its traditional arguments for God's existence express a 'demand of
reason' that reality must be a whole. This claim would defeat itself
if we supposed it could be wholly met at the rational level: the
furthest we may go without undermining the argument for transcendence itself is a purely formal knowledge of some ultimate
ground or principle of reality of whose nature we can form no proper
conception. As Father Herbert McCabe O.P. has summed up the
character of this theology of God's relation to the world: 'Broadly
speaking, we look at the world and it has a created look about it.'[22]
No satisfactory epistemological basis here for our grasp of the living
God as one who enters into communication with man. Yet on the
other hand, to claim that we have some strictly immediate knowledge of God seems futile. It seems absurd to claim a transcendent
experience of God, for part of the meaning of 'transcendent' is
precisely 'what goes beyond experience'. But if there can be no
strictly immediate knowledge of God, how can some direct but
mediate knowledge of him be claimed without presupposing such
a power to determine his nature as would deny his transcendence?[23]
Once again, the aesthetic model may assist us.

What the artwork mediates to us is a particular reality in its
depth. It sheds light on that reality exactly in the mystery of its
being. Professor Hywel Lewis has written:

> The more the artist invests the commonplace realities of ordinary
> experience with his peculiar individual impression of them, the
> more starkly do they present to him an irreducibly other nature.
> The closer the artist moves towards reality in his art the more
> is it alarmingly aloof. Paradoxically but unmistakeably, there is
> in art an unveiling which is at the same time a concealment. In
> the very process of clarification there is also a deepening of

mystery. Mystery that is not in the sense that there is a mystery at the end of every scientific truth, the sense, that is, that the solution of problems sets us *ad infinitum* new problems to solve, but in a more absolute and immediate sense that that which is made peculiarly plain to us is itself proportionately more enigmatic. Mystery and illumination are one in art.[24]

The artist's form, concrete, particular, given, cataphatic, yields up to us a meaning which is inexhaustible, mysterious and apophatic. Lewis concludes that

> the vision which the artist has is . . . always on the point of passing over into a religious one, for in having the individual character of things displayed in the strangeness and mystery of their being just what they are, in being caught up in their finality in the impact they make in art, we are impinging closely on the ultimate mystery of all things in the inevitability of their having a transcendent source.[25]

It is fitting to leave the last word in this chapter to that contemporary 'father of the Church' Hans Urs von Balthasar who has done more than anyone to nurture a theological aesthetics, drawing out of oblivion the theme of glory that will save us from what Jürgen Moltmann has called, 'seeing the meaning of life only in being useful and being used'.[25] In his *Verbum Caro*, von Balthasar concludes an exposition of the theology of revelation with these words,

> Revelation itself is the foundation of a dialectic, of ever increasing range and intensity, between event and vision. The element of the divinely tremendous – inherent in the event itself – first overwhelms the person contemplating it, so much so that no way remains open to him except that of simple discipleship, and this in turn brings a new sense of being overwhelmed, but this time at a deeper level. This dialectic, however, is in need of a genuine *structure* if it is to be conformable to man and the world. Only such a structure brings out clearly the background of infinite mystery that seeks to reveal itself as the beautiful, true and good. In its absence, faith would not be in conformity with human nature but spiritualistic and irrational. The historical revelation

is moulded throughout into a single structure so that the person contemplating it perceives, through the relationships and proportion of its various parts, the divine rightness of the whole. However clear and convincing these relations are they are none the less inexhaustible – not merely in practical experience (because we lack the power to grasp them in their entirety), but also in principle, because what comes to light in the structure is something which opens our minds to the infinite.[27]

CHAPTER EIGHT

Sketch for a Christology of the Image

In a christology situated within an aesthetic theology of revelation such as this essay has described it, revelation in Christ will be the perception of the form of Jesus Christ as the appearing amongst us of God's own transcendent reality. To say that there is divine revelation in and through the figure of Jesus, then, will be to invite someone to approach Christ on the model of the artwork as disclosing a new dimension to human life and death. This artwork of Christ clarifies the meaning of all human existence and yet does so by a radiance issuing from a figure who, contemplated in himself, is all the more mysterious. As St Mark's Gospel presents the matter, Jesus was experienced both as in the midst of and as always ahead of his disciples.[1]

Jesus, the Revealer of the Father

Following Aristotle's dictum that the pursuit of understanding moves through the more familiar to the less, let us begin from 'below', from the human and the historical. A christology starting from this point will be concerned to explore what is given to us in the figure of the man Jesus and to relate that to our sense of God. In terms of the model of the artwork, christology considers the 'iconic' quality of Jesus' life and death, asking what this man communicates to us of the divine. The Christian claim for the significance of Jesus may be put in the manner of the man who has grasped the meaning of the artwork and sums up for others the effects of aesthetic experience. This human icon, we might say, 'extends the horizons of perception', and 'lets us see the world in a way we never have before'. It 'allows us to know the artist', and 'moves and transforms us in our very depth'.[2] What features of the

119

life and death of Jesus belong to his 'aesthetic' reality, his being a 'significant form' that discloses a fresh world of meaning to us?

We have noted whilst considering Paul's 'Adam' typology that, in the distance from the historical Jesus by which Paul could stand back and contemplate the form of his life, it was above all Jesus' obedience to death out of love which shaped the significant form wherein he could be seen as the disclosure of God.[3] Jesus in his life and death rendered palpable the love, mercy, and fidelity of God in the medium of a human life, and in particular in freely chosen weakness, humbling of self and an extremity of self-giving. For Paul, as Professor A. T. Hanson has insisted, 'the weakness shown in the crucifixion is really divine strength. The secret is manifested in the resurrection.'[4]

The Christianity which Paul offers is 'God's wisdom *in a mystery*'. It is the divine present in a fragile ambiguity which calls for the most strenuous sensitivity if it is to be recognized for what it is. The Roman and Jewish rulers of Palestine during Jesus' lifetime, the men who presided over his execution, and behind them the angelic powers later Jewish thinkers believed bound up with political authority, totally lacked the ability to discern the divine content in the lowly form they saw in Jesus.

> None of the rulers of this age understood this; for if they had, they would not have crucified the Lord of glory.[5]

Hanson comments appropriately:

> It was not that the divinity lay hid behind the humanity, like the hook hidden in the bait in the famous patristic simile. Rather the powers failed to recognise that the humanity ('the weakness of God') revealed God's nature. . . . Paul puts it in soteriological terms: they failed to recognise God's wonderful design. But if you are to speak in terms of revelation, as you must, you have to say that they failed to recognise God's very nature revealed in the humanity of Christ.[6]

For the historical Jesus to be glimpsed as such an icon or disclosure of the divine the New Testament sources must yield up some definite features for us to focus on. The Christ of faith must be located and earthed in the history of Jesus, for the meaning of the 'Kingdom of God' he proclaimed was creatively constructed by him in the course of his ministry. If the historical figure of Jesus is in no sense recoverable, there is nothing for theologically aesthetic perception to work upon. I would suggest that Paul's impressionist portrait of Jesus, his attempt to capture 'the essential gestures' of his life, is adequately supported in the primitive gospel tradition. The ministry of Jesus, his humble service of men carried out within an utterly confident proclamation of the unconditional love and mercy of God towards them, itself disclosed the Kingdom of his Father of which Jesus spoke. The crucifixion, with its twin marks of forgiveness of the guilty by the innocent and triumphant trust in that Father's unsurpassable power, was the highpoint of this ministry and therefore of this disclosure. In both we are presented with a consistent, coherent form of life, where everything is of a piece and carries the unmistakeable mark of a personal style. If we read this artwork aright, we may see it as the disclosure of God to us, for the qualities of the divine subject *represented* in the person of Jesus are actually *presented* by this design of his life.

The nineteenth century liberal quest for the historical Jesus foundered on the discovery that there was no North-west Passage to be charted that would bypass the apostolic preaching of the early Church and bring us directly to the man as he had lived. Every attempted re-routing left us with a purely 'cypher' figure who simply reflected the presuppositions or ideals of the historian's own time or choosing. But in the 1950s a new quest opened up in which scholars at last accepted the limitations of their source materials open-eyed and even enthusiastically for they had hit upon a new and distinctly promising principle of research.[7] The principle is a simple one. There must surely be elements in what the Church proclaimed about Christ which can suggest how that proclamation came about, how the Jesus of history could be presented convincingly as the Christ of faith. To suppose that no such filaments of connection exist is to introduce a massive and unwarrantable rupture into the nexus of cause and effect in historical explanation. Professor C. F. D. Moule calls the model on which the best of this new corpus of interpretation operates the model of development. The new quest exhibits to us various stages in the development of perception about Jesus, stages straddles across the supreme dividing-line of the Easter experience. These stages, he writes,

> are analogous not so much to the emergence of a new species, as to the unfolding (if you like) of flower from bud and the growth of fruit from flower . . . (although) even in so continuous a process as the opening of a bud into a flower, plenty of extraneous matter is absorbed. Metabolism in a living thing is never a completely self-contained process, like the mere springing open of a Japanese paper flower when it is dropped into water.[8]

The use of fresh language and concepts in communicating the Christian faith within the New Testament period, in other words, by no means wholly obliterates an earlier configuration issuing from Jesus himself, as he struck his own contemporaries. We may look, in and beneath the various New Testament documents, not for a detailed biography of the life of Jesus such as the old quest sought (this is impossible from the nature of the records), but for some grasp of the fundamental structure of his life.

Positive and exciting results have been obtained by working out from the data of Jesus' gestures, his enacted parables as the gospel tradition records these in a cheerful variety of contexts. Jesus had wished to be understood on the basis of a pattern of actions of which extending table-fellowship to prostitutes and Quisling tax-collectors is perhaps the most instructive example. As Dr. F. W. Dillistone has put it,

> Amidst all that is uncertain in any effort to reconstruct a picture of the historical Jesus, one . . . characteristic of his earthly career has gained wide recognition as being genuine and authentic. He ate and drank with tax-collectors and sinners. . . . References to this aspect of his ministry occur in diverse contexts in the synoptic gospels and the analysis of 'forms' in the gospel tradition has revealed the fact that these references are to be found in many patterns and are recorded, it would appear, with varying motivations. In other words, the criticism of the narratives reveals no single conscious purpose for drawing attention in these various passages to this particular aspect of Jesus' ministry. If there is one pattern of his earthly activity which can be regarded

as supported by a remarkable cluster of converging evidences it is his going forth to seek and to save that which was lost.[9]

In such table-fellowship in the houses of social outcastes and religious excommunicates Jesus provided a series of vignettes of the Kingdom of God. These miniatures opened up a dimension of depth in people's lives in which the presence of the love and mercy of God could be experienced. 'The whole implication is that the joys of the final Messianic banquet were already being experienced as men and women responded to Jesus' outstretched hand of friendship'.[10] The thaumaturgical acts of Jesus, his miracles and exorcisms, wherever these may be allowed an historical basis, should be placed in the same perspective. The poor, the weak, and the sick experience here and now symbolically the goodness and power of God so that they can bear witness of it to others. All such actions by Jesus are done not simply for their own sake, although of course they are worth doing in the simplest human terms, but for their parabolic value as signs of a greater healing, nourishment, and liberation than the purely literal and matter-of-fact. They point to God as 'saviour', healer, of the whole human condition. The concern for enemies and outcastes which formed the central and deliberate purpose of the life of Jesus came to its climax and consummation on the cross as the Passion narratives of the Gospels testify.[11] It was perhaps the enacted parables of the life which enabled the disciples to see this death of the Master, apparently a merely passive affair, a *passio*, something undergone, as itself a divine action. The death belonged to and crowned the sequence of scenes in which he had taught them to see the quality of God's mercy disclosed.

All these significant actions of Jesus belong together in a single narrative sequence. First of all, the temporal character of all human life implies such a narrative structure. Secondly, Jesus' own adoption of a mission, signified in his baptism at the hands of John, another irrefragible piece of historical bed-rock, entails that the meaning of his life may be found in an end or goal, to which his actions convergently direct our gaze. It is this narrative sequence of scenes, sustained throughout the Gospels and unfolded in the christological developments of the New Testament theologians, which gives us a form for Jesus' life that is irradiated by God's transcendence. There is much in respect of Jesus' symbolization of the Kingdom that still remains in debate. For some, the 'Son of Man' sayings express Jesus' primary symbol for his vocation; for others, this is later language that at best expresses a perception of some aspect of the original form. But we have foundations secure enough to claim right of access to the historical reality of the narrative art of Jesus, by which he showed himself as the truly selfless man who engages with evil to serve the world.

The meaning of this narrative art of 'The Way of the Lord' has been evoked by Ethelbert Stauffer under three headings which correspond to this last characterizing of Jesus' imaginative self-presentation. First of all, he is the one who exists only to point to Another:

> The doxological understanding looks to the relation between Christ and God. Jesus was sent to reveal and accomplish the *gloria Dei* in the midst of a world that, intoxicated with its own self-glorification, hears and wants to hear nothing further about God's glory. But he can only fulfil his mission if his own glory means nothing to him, and God's glory all. Hence the son of man has nowhere to lay his head. So he meets the disciples' confession that he is the Messiah with a saying about his passion. And so he goes from the mount of transfiguration on his way of self-renunciation to the cross of Golgotha. The life of Jesus is an acted doxology.

Secondly, he engages in combat with evil in all its spawning forms:

> The antagonistic conception of the Way of Christ considers the relation between him and the devil. The life of the son of man is a continual fight with the demonic prince of this world and all who are in his service.

Lastly, he is the Servant:

> The soteriological interpretation of the Way of the Lord deals with the relation between Christ and the world. His life is spent and fulfilled in this service to the world. He submits to the baptism of those who are burdened with sin, so as to fulfil his

mission as the bearer of others' burdens, and so as to remove the sin that burdened many.[12]

This 'Way of the Lord' in its threefold meaning is, Stauffer would hold, unfolded and perfected in the christology of the New Testament.

This form of life, recontextualized and seen in a new radiance after the resurrection appearances, opened up a fresh world of meaning for the disciples. Dwelling in this world of meaning, they found themselves contemplating a unique design of human life which presented them with God himself as subject. In aesthetic terms, design is what presents content, or subject. I take two examples from artworks themselves suggested by the Passion of Jesus. In El Greco's *The Agony in the Garden*, qualities of the design in the distorted rocks twisted out of true and in the menacing cloud-shapes in the upper part of the painting present the emotional qualities with which El Greco sees Christ burdened at Gethsemane. In Georges Rouault's *Christ Mocked by Soldiers*, the construction of the picture space, where the soldiers' faces crowd the head of Jesus, and the electric quality of the texture, its strong hues framed by black lines, both convey the extreme pressure beneath which Jesus is bowed – yet also the simultaneous intensity of purpose with which he accepts his humiliation. Analogously, the basic design of the life of Jesus enables us to apprehend the quality of God. God is now seen as the glorious love which wills to enter into and transform the condition of man.

Certainly this new sense of God is derivable from the artwork of Christ not as an isolated *oeuvre* but rather when Jesus is seen in continuity with the wider iconology of creation and of the Old Testament. Without these it makes no sense to speak of recognizing *God* in Jesus. The living icon of Jesus is not successful artistic communication unless it is set, as any image or set of images must be, within a tradition of iconology. The most novel and revolutionary images always presuppose inherited meanings, or they could not speak to us at all. The first disciples saw the form of his existence standing out from such a wider iconology – from the salvation history of the Jewish people, as well as from that commerce of man with the created cosmos to which so many of his parables refer us. Without this pattern of images, including most importantly the

125

prophetic and mediatorial figures I have mentioned in discussing the theomorphic view of man in the Old Testament, the image Jesus presented could scarcely have been recognized as bearing the marks of the grace and truth of God.[13] On the other hand, it is this image which finally confers on all the others their true significance and coherence.

> In the life, death and resurrection of Jesus Christ, these characteristics were thrown into strong relief, so that Jesus Christ acted as a screen through which only what was true and authentic in God's nature penetrated to the apprehension of christians.[14]

Jesus, then, is both recognizable as the supreme image and revelation of God through indebtedness to this wider iconology, and also acts himself as the decisive criterion for the accurate perception of God in Israel's history. The inter-relation and inter-penetration of these two movements of perception may be seen in the various 'titles' of Jesus drawn from Old Testament sources in the New Testament (Messiah, King, Lamb of God, High Priest, and so forth)[15] and in the summaries of the first apostolic preaching in the Book of the Acts.[16]

In the narrative structure of this art, the cross, I have said, forms the climax and consummation. The earliest Christian preaching centred on the meaning of the death of Christ, the victorious passion whose triumphant expression is the resurrection. This should bring us to consider the crucifix as the figure wherein design and subject cohere most fully together. The words and deeds of Jesus become fully intelligible for the first time in the light of this sign. His demand for total obedience and a radical re-orientation of life must be heard while within the visual range of the image of the crucified, since this expresses the infinite love of God which makes sense of the demand in the first place. We have seen in our survey of patristic materials that Maximus the Confessor had placed the iconic quality of life of Christ in his *love*.[17] In this century the Swiss theologian Hans Urs von Balthasar has constructed a christology strongly Maximian in tenor, on the two poles of charity and the perception of the divine glory.[18] The splendour of an object, Balthasar points out, only attracts the beholder by some form of eros, a pull of desire. Conversely, the object we love always appears to us wonderful and

126

glorious. Revelation in Christ brings these two poles, love and beauty, into a unity. The Fourth Gospel describes the person of Jesus as radiant with 'mercy and steadfast love' and at the same time proclaims him as the communication of God's glory, tabernacling with his people as the glory of Yahweh had been said to do in time past by the Priestly School:

> We saw his glory, the glory that is his as the only Son of the Father, full of grace and truth.[19]

This has been expressed many times in a painterly way in the history of Christian iconography. The figure of the dead Christ is set against a gold background of paint or mosaic, as in the great twelfth-century apse mosaic of the aureoled Christ, crucified on the Tree of Life, in the Dominican church of San Clemente in Rome.

But *can* a dying man spreadeagled on a gibbet thus disclose to us a world of divine significance? The model of the artwork should suggest a possibility at least. The fact that the stuff of Jesus' existence was made up of the common materials of all human life, the ordinary chemistry of the human body and brain, the ordinary psychology of the dynamic structures of the human mind, the ordinary history of acquisition of concepts, perceptions, and images mediated through the tissue of a particular society and culture does not argue that such a transcendent significance cannot attach to a human life and death any more than the fact that, say, Edvard Munch's *The Sun* is made up of canvas, pigment, and oil prevents it from being an aesthetic disclosure, unforgettable in its intensity, of the terrifying energies of nature. It is in the nature of form that by means of it matter takes on a significance of an order beyond itself. The significance really attaches to the form; it is not available to us by some independent mental path and merely hooked on to form as a convenient peg for memory.

> Just as in love I encounter the other *as* the other in all his freedom, and am confronted by something which I cannot dominate in any sense, so in the aesthetic sphere, it is impossible to attribute the form which presents itself to a fiction of my imagination. In both cases the 'understanding' of that which reveals

itself cannot be subsumed under categories of knowledge which imply control.[20]

To dissolve the power of form into some supposed structure of human mental awareness is simply to betray the fact that the specific quality of the splendour of form has never been felt. The artwork itself, Gadamer would say, takes priority over the aesthetic consciousness. The icon of Christ, then, is irreplaceably significant in our knowledge of God. A retrospective glance at what we have established about the shape of the artwork will remind us why this is so. Art is essentially a reality which opens out onto other realities while remaining permanently necessary for our grasp of those realities. The artwork can never be surpassed as the altogether wonderful medium of the peculiar knowledge it grants us.[21] Hence, in the case of Jesus, what Dr Karl Rahner speaks of as 'the eternal significance of the humanity of Christ'.[22]

Without this image the 'negative theology' of our approach to the God who is always more unlike than he is like finite reality is in danger of drifting off into atheism or agnosticism, or some philosophy or mysticism of identity. But here, where the concrete form of revelation in Christ stands before us, the wholly other and ever greater God appears and grasps us in the very act of overwhelming us by his incomprehensible love. It is only through form that the splendour of the everlasting Beauty of God can shine out. That is the Beauty we posit as the reality of the Artist glimpsed in the style of innumerable images both in cosmic nature and also in those human figures who have expressed God's pathos towards the world, as these are decisively re-interpreted by the image of God in Christ. Expressed in aesthetic terms the charismatic and ecstatic experience which, historically, has marked the Christian Church both in its first generation and then sporadically at many times and places since is the effect of human perception being seized and transported by the 'splendour of form' of God which appeared in Christ.

Something which has existed since the beginning,
that we have heard,
and *we have seen with our own eyes;*
that *we have watched*
and touched with our hands:

the Word, who is life
this is our subject.
That life was made visible
we saw it and we are giving our testimony
telling you of the eternal life which was with the Father
and has been made *visible* to us.
What we have seen and heard
we are telling you,
so that you too may be in union with us,
as we are in union with the Father,
and with his Son Jesus Christ.
We are writing this to you to make our own *joy* complete.[23]

From the same school as this First Letter of St John comes the Fourth Gospel, that extended, theologically contemplative interpretation of the significance of Christ which is the master-work of the Johannine writers. Although the Synoptic tradition uses from time to time the language of adoration or obeisance (*proskunein*) for men's response to the figure of Jesus, suggesting a numinous presence already recognized during his ministry, it is St John's Gospel above all which identifies rapture before the man Jesus with rapture before the glory of God. In the encounter with Jesus the contours of his unique silhouette detach themselves in such a way that suddenly the light of the Unconditioned can pierce a man through, bringing him to his knees in the gesture of *proskunesis* before Christ and making him a disciple. At one point John describes how Jesus heals a blind man in the streets of Jerusalem in the context of mounting opposition to his ministry. A second encounter takes place in which a new depth to Jesus' being is disclosed. The man has been victimized for his mere association with the Master, so

Jesus heard that they had driven him away, and when he found him he said to him, 'Do you believe in the Son of Man?' 'Sir', the man replied, 'Tell me who he is so that I may believe in him.' Jesus said, 'You are looking at him; he is speaking to you.' The man said 'Lord, I believe', and worshipped him (*prosekunesen auto*).[24]

Some exegetes will protest that the Fourth Gospel, just because it

129

is a highly wrought theological exposition of the significance of Jesus, cannot be used to reconstruct the reaction of his own contemporaries to him. These exegetes would include A. T. Hanson, even though he admits that we cannot assume there were 'no intimations of divinity in Jesus' life before the resurrection. The disciples could not so soon have come to so exalted a view of him after the resurrection had they not recognised something divine in him during his historical existence'.[25] But the most balanced view of the vexed question of the historicity of John's Gospel sees it as a montage of remembered situations in the life of Jesus and contemporary situations in the life of the early Church. John shows a determination to witness to both the historical tradition about Jesus and the contemporary implications of that witness – without letting either do violence to the other.[26] In John's reporting of this gesture, and in the comparable remarks of the Synoptics it is the fact that the homage is paid to Jesus by strict monotheists which is utterly startling.[27]

Jesus, the Son of God

It is at this point, with the recognition that Jesus is a man in whom God is embodied, as meaning in the artwork, that our christological exploration 'from below' reaches the end of its usefulness. If we are brought by looking at the life of Jesus to see him as the form of God's love appearing in the world, and if we then see the divine meaning that he embodies as at once utterly his own and utterly God's we can do nothing but concede that his personal identity must somehow go back into the life of God himself. And here we cannot allow ourselves the luxury of mythopoeic expressions. The ancient dramas of God's relations with men wove their tales in terms of a plurality of semi-divine figures who express the commerce and relationship between man and the divine. But with that clarity of perception that Israel's long struggle with the pagan environment and with her own temptations to divinize her own life and achievement gives to those who know of the Judaic criticism of the world of myth, we have to say that what is not God is not divine, what is not the Uncreated is the created. And at this point we stand on the edge of 'christology from above'. For what can it mean to say that

Jesus' person is self-identical with God himself? Christology from above is the attempt to speak sense about the majesty in the form of Christ which exacts from the beholder the attitude of *adoration*, given that God is God and man is man.

Recovering the teaching of the Priestly School, glanced at earlier on how man is God's 'image' because he is created by God with the capacity to disclose the divine, will throw light, I suggest, on this perennial problem of christology which came into sharpest relief with the formulation of the mystery of Christ at Chalcedon. For there the catholic Church solemnly bound itself to

teach men to acknowledge one and the same Son, our Lord Jesus Christ, at once complete in Godhead and complete in manhood, truly God and truly man consisting also of a reasonable soul and body; of one substance with the Father as regards his Godhead, and at the same time of one substance with us as regards his manhood; like us in all respects, apart from sin; as regards his Godhead, begotten of the Father before the ages, but yet as regards his manhood begotten, for us men and for our salvation, of Mary the Virgin, the Godbearer; one and the same Christ, Son, Lord, Only-begotten, recognized in two natures, without confusion, without change, without division, without separation; the distinction of natures being in no way annulled by the union, but rather the characteristics of each nature being preserved and coming together to form one person and subsistence, not as parted or separated into two persons, but one and the same Son, and Only-begotten God the Word, Lord Jesus Christ. . . .[28]

How are we today to understand this lapidary statement of the implications of the gesture of prostration by that disciple of Jesus? The life of faith-seeking-understanding atrophies if there is not a constant attempt to restate in fuller and more satisfactory ways the credal formulae of the past.

The clearest formulations, the most sanctified formulas, the classic condensations of the centuries-long work of the Church in prayer, reflexion and struggle concerning God's mysteries: all these derive their life from the fact that they are not end but beginning, not goal but means, truths which open the way to the

– ever greater – Truth. . . . Every formula transcends itself (not because it is false but precisely because it is true).[29]

Taking up the challenge which Rahner lays down here to all who would venture to speak of the Church's faith, will the theological resources surveyed in this essay help us to articulate the interrelation of the divine and the human in Jesus Christ?

Just as Anglican and Reformed divines in our day have made public their doubts whether the Chalcedonian definition can yield a 'reasoned account of Christ as both fully human and fully divine' and voiced their suspicion that in any difficulty it is the humanity of Christ which has suffered, so Catholic theologians too have been sensitive to the need for a convincing and credible re-pristinization of the Church's dogmatic vision of Jesus. J.-J. Latour has gone to the heart of the matter by asking:

> Can one conceive of the union of natures as so intimate that it transforms, while preserving, the human interiority of Christ by its mark? Or does the union have to be understood in such a way that the divine cannot be disclosed at all by the human nature as such, so that inescapably we need to invoke instead a privileged and essentially supernatural beatific vision?[30]

In other words, can we commend the Chalcedonian definition by showing how the revelatory significance of Jesus can be rooted in the actuality of his own being, as the God-man, without overthrowing the humanity which, as we have seen, is the medium of his revelatory value? Is there some element in *humanity* which might indicate how Jesus can be in the actual structures of his personal constitution, identical with God, and know himself as the only-begotten Son of the Father? For it seems to be the case that had Jesus been capable of attaining immediately and directly to the divine root of his existence as man, we could hardly say with the Council of Chalcedon that he is 'consubstantial with us according to his humanity'. He would not be held within the boundaries of properly human existence at all in such a case. It is part of the constitution of finite spiritual creatures such as ourselves that no particular content of awareness ever gives us access to our own ultimate identity or exhausts the mystery of the 'I' at the root of our being. *A fortiori* such an experience would be alien to the human if the 'I' grasped in the self-consciousness of Jesus were the 'I' of divine creativity itself. And yet the New Testament evidence that Jesus saw the 'Kingdom' of his Father breaking in with his own mission, presence and personal relations with others, invites us to make some such connection between the Jesus who makes that proclamation about his Father and the Christ who is proclaimed to be God's very self-expression, Word, and Son by the Church. Indeed, if Jesus were wholly without any realization of his ultimate identity then incarnation would be an unthinkable monstrosity. Perhaps the theology of the image can suggest a way through this impasse by locating man's essence in his *relatedness to God*.

Man images God in so far as there is a real presence in the human spirit, embodied as that is in the world, of God's own 'pathos'.[31] The openness of man to God which permits him to express the divine is what is most characteristically human in him.[32] Now for orthodox christological doctrine, the Logos of God, the ultimate identity of Jesus, is himself pure relation to the Father.[33] He has no other reality than this relation. The self-awareness of the Word Incarnate then cannot be simply self-contained and self-referring, for he has no autonomous existence on which awareness can be brought to bear. In Christ's humanity the hypostatic union is not a content which he might at any moment advert to by reflection. If the Logos, the divine reality of that union, is wholly turned towards the Father, the union itself must be some new being-in-relation towards the personal source of the Godhead. And if man's capacity to embody the pathos of God gives him what is most properly his own then it is possible to think that this existence of 'filial love turned towards the Father' which is God's Word might be expressed in the form of a human life and a human self-awareness – without impairing their integrity.

> The person is a relational being. More particularly, the person of the Son is a relation to the Father. . . . When the Son humanly takes consciousness of himself, he does it as a Son, by taking consciousness of his relation to the Father. . . . Jesus does not behave like a man who in a mysterious manner feels or sees God but as a son who has the most intimate knowledge of the Father.[34]

133

In this case, the hypostatic union can be said not to disrupt the structure of man's being, but on the contrary to bring it to its full realization, albeit in a unique way.

It seems strange, therefore, that A. T. Hanson in a study cited several times in this book should judge the Pauline vision of God disclosed in the humanity of Jesus to lie on quite another 'trajectory' or line of development from the teaching of Chalcedon. Orthodox christology is very far from saying that the humanity of Jesus is an encumbrance to his revealing of God. When Chalcedon speaks of the single divine 'person', hypostasis, or prosopon in Christ, it does not use that term in its modern psychological sense at all. It is not alleging that there is no human personality in Jesus, in the sense of an empirical but stable, coherent and distinctive assemblage of traits and habits. To say that in Jesus there is no hypostasis apart from the divine Son is simply to say that insofar as God the Son in his love for men chose to enter human history, he was and is the man Jesus. Thus the words, acts, and experiences of that man are not simply the instruments of the eternal saving power of God the Son: they *are* that saving power projected into human history. Jesus precisely in his full humanity is God the Son, the Saviour.[35]

The incarnation raises the Old Testament aesthetic ontology of man in the image of God to a new intensity. The Word Incarnate serves as a visual language for God at an incomparably higher power than do the prophets. Now we have explored the track of 'christology from above' let us return to Rahner's phrase about the 'eternal significance of the humanity of Christ' with the new interest which discovery of the identity of our relation to Christ the Image with our relation to God as the ultimate ground and meaning of the world should evidently give us. We may pick up his essay at the point where he is talking about a dialectic of affirmation and negation in the knowledge of God. We are familiar with the theme because we have earlier found here part of the significance of the artwork for man's grasp of revelation. Rahner writes:

We may speak about the impersonal Absolute without the non-absolute flesh of the Son, but the personal Absolute can be truly found only in him, in whom dwells the fullness of the Godhead in the earthly vessel of his humanity. Without him every absolute of which we speak or which we imagine we attain by mystical flight is in the last analysis merely the never attained, objective correlate of that empty and hollow, dark and despairingly self-consuming infinity which we are ourselves: the infinity of dissatisfied finiteness, but not the blessed infinity of truly limitless fullness. This, however, can be found only where Jesus of Nazareth is, this finite concrete being, this contingent being, who remains in all eternity. . . . Jesus, the Man, not merely was at one time of decisive importance for our salvation . . . but as the one who became man and has remained a creature – he is now and for all eternity the permanent openness of our finite being to the living God of infinite, eternal life.[36]

But if Christ on Calvary is the Image and Expression and Exegesis of God, we are still left with the question of how our hearts may see him with clear vision. And this is where we must trace the relation of the metaphor of the image to the theology of faith, the subjective component in revelation. The artwork opens up the world, including the world of God, but requires for this the liberation of the perceptive powers of man.

CHAPTER NINE

The Eyes of Faith

The events which constitute the revelation of God in Jesus Christ are complex events for they take place as a fusion of two elements, subject and object. They involve a reality we are presented with, and a response by which we become present to that reality. In this they can stake out no special claims to distinction. All events have this character, even those studied by the natural scientist for he too makes a certain contribution as observer to what he observes. In the Christian tradition, however, the subjective component in the revelatory event does at least possess a special name. Appropriate subjective response to revelation, grasping its transcendent, inexhaustible significance in the particular, concrete form in which it appears, is otherwise termed *faith*. An aesthetic theology can help us to elucidate the nature of this faith-response.

In classical Christian thought, faith is the source both of contemplative and mystical insight into God on the one hand, and the life of charity in practical action on the other. It is not something confined within the brief moment when we make an initial response to some further dimension we have glimpsed in Jesus. Rather, it extends throughout the Christian life as the constitutive feature of the knowing and loving which is distinctive of that life. To read the significance of the artwork of Christ is to be transformed oneself, so that in one's own turn one may express the divine pathos in a continuing communion with God *via* his image. We discover a quite gratuitous possibility of being transported and raised up into the world which the form reveals. This unsuspected gift of a power to reform self by a subtle but crucial shifting of all one's perceptions is what is meant by speaking of the 'grace' of faith. Hans Urs von Balthasar in the opening volume of his *Herrlichkeit*, 'Seeing the Form', traces the dialectic of subjective and objective evidence in revelation by showing how our perception of the form of the divine

136

in the human is always intimately related to the transforming power of the content of that form upon us.[1]

Von Balthasar remarks that in art form strikes us as splendid because the delight it arouses is grounded on the deep truth and goodness of the reality which shows and offers itself there as something infinitely precious and fascinating. If we really perceive the form, we see it not just as a detached *Gestalt*, a sensuous configuration, but as *Glanz*, radiance, the glory of being. In contemplating the form we are 'entranced' and 'ravished' by this depth which appears in and through it. Von Balthasar recognizes that we have here a most useful analogy for the revelatory event. He sets by its side the great Nativity Preface in the Mass of the Roman Rite:

> By the mystery of the Word made flesh
> the light of your glory has shone afresh
> upon the eyes of our mind, so that while
> we acknowledge him to be God seen by men
> we may be drawn by him to the love of things
> unseen.

God empowers the 'eyes of our mind' with a new 'light' so that we can recognize in a visual medium an object which is God himself, communicated through the sacramental mystery of the form of the Word Incarnate. In this vision there is, further, a 'rapture' which carries us from the visible to the invisible reality made present in its sign, Jesus Christ. In speaking of the grace of faith we find ourselves offering an account of how man discovers the form of the self-revealing God. But this discovery is never made without evoking a progressive transformation of the person who thereby receives the eyes to see the divine image pointing ever more clearly away from itself to the invisible God. In all sound aesthetics, according to Balthasar, the doctrine of the perception of the beautiful and the doctrine of its ravishing power are ordered to each other. No one truly perceives without this self-transcending, ec-static element of rapture. The phrase 'the light of faith', then, must needs carry an ambiguity: the glory of God in Christ can be seen only by the eyes of faith but the eyes of faith can only see when the light of faith falls on them from the divine form of Jesus Christ. The ambiguity is an

137

inbuilt one, just as in looking at pictures a humbling of self before the object is both a condition and an effect of really seeing.

The notion that perception and transformation are vitally inter-linked in art is an organizing feature in the aesthetic writings of Mikel Dufrenne, on whom this essay has drawn more than once. Aesthetic feeling is deep, according to Dufrenne, because the aes-thetic object reaches into everything that makes a man a perceiver of meaning. We do not need to be Breton peasants bowed to the ground with toil in order to understand Gauguin's *The Yellow Christ*, nor mothers to grasp a Henry Moore *Madonna and Child*. The work itself will show us what it is to stoop in sacrifice towards the earth, or how mother and baby are a profound unity – but only on the condition that we *participate* in the artwork through that in us which is capable of being affected by it. There is a facet of this response evoked by a painting which, Dufrenne thinks, can only be called *love*. For, he asks, 'Is not love that expectation of a conversion by the attention we pay to the other, to what he is and expresses?'[2] In theological terms, we look to the saints and the mystics, to men whose minds are in love with God, to find out what subjective response to revelation, at its most searching and complete might conceivably be like. In essence, it is humility, the readiness to accept the gift of the divine love as it is, in the necessity and rightness of form it has. Far from being, then, a pejoratively subjective enthusi-asm, emotive, self-indulgent, self-referential, and intellectually dis-honest, perception of the form of God in Jesus can only be developed by constant and demanding attention to the image in all its otherness.

With this we may compare some words of a commentator on the art of the icon who has experienced this art in the context of worship rather than that of the gallery:

Its holy personages come forth ready to bless and liberate – ready to convert the beholder from his restricted and limited point of view to the full view of their spiritual vision. For the art of the icon is ultimately so to transform the person who moves towards it that he no longer distinguishes between the worlds of eternity and time, of spirit and matter, of the divine and the human, but sees both as one reality, both as aspects of that

138

unaged and ageless Light in which all things live, move and have their being.[3]

Philip Sherrard in this lyrical passage is not attempting a precise theological formulation. But his conviction that the signs of art can touch us in such a way that we come to be increasingly in communication and communion with what they signify challenges us to take the artwork seriously as a 'range of comparison' for the structure of faith. As we have seen, the notion that reading the significance of the artwork is transformative of the perceiver is fully Pauline.[4] Its presence in later Christian tradition accounts for the at first sight confusing way the Fathers and others use image language both for the theology of the incarnation as God's self-revelation in Christ, and for the theology of faith as our response to that disclosure.[5] To look more closely at just how this 'transfiguration by grace' operates I want to turn to one particular witness in the history of theology. Before that, however, let us briefly recapitulate our conclusions so far.

One of the virtues of the model of the artwork for the theology of revelation is that it allows us a very ample and generous idea of the objectivity of revelation. The artwork is the taking up of prior materials – paint, canvas, stone; shapes and colours; primary symbols and stylistic conventions – into a new configuration of meaning which the artwork carries as its own immanent significance. It is in its very 'thinghood' the source of power to reinterpret our experience.' But while it is true that God in Christ has taken up the materials of a human physiology and a human culture into a form which is the embodiment of his own self-expression, we still need to do justice to the subjective facet of revelation, our perception of the significance of Christ:

The Church holds that the Christ of faith is identical with Jesus of Nazareth and that he, having really lived among men, is a historical figure. But she is immediately concerned with Jesus *as* the Christ, the revelation of God. . . . There is no revelation apart from subjects who receive it. The revelation effected in Jesus implies not only the presence of God in him, but also the recognition of that presence by those who were the witnesses of his life. It is in the faith of the apostles and the original Christian

139

community that Jesus has actually become the revelation of God for humanity as a whole.[6]

This subjective aspect of revelation continues, of course, whenever men attain to God through the sign of Jesus. As Canon Jean Mouroux has insisted there is a characteristic 'Christian experience' which

> on all sides extends beyond 'experience' in the empiricist sense of that word. The problem of Christian experience lies in the attempt to define a 'structured *élan*' whose power of re-orientation (grace) and whose attracting pole (the triune God) are purely spiritual and supernatural, and which draws man's whole being, with all his activities and passivities, the most spiritual and the most sensuous, towards God. . . .[7]

This is the point at which the theology of the Word Incarnate and the theology of faith meet and embrace each other. Here, too, aesthetics may help us to organize the data of our subject, for the experience of art seems to exhibit an analogous power to precipitate us into a new grasp of the real, far beyond what we could have envisaged before we stood before the artwork. To see a piece of organized material as an artwork is already to make some kind of aesthetic response. Yet it is perfectly possible to recognize that Rembrandt's *Christ Preaching to the Poor* is what English language users call an art-object, without opening yourself to the full disclosure of significance which the painting can give. To reach that disclosure requires a contemplative perception, an 'élan' called forth by an obscure but certain sense of the plenitude of meaning the painting carries, but an *élan* which is 'structured', that is, which is controlled and ordered by the objective form perceived in the artwork, not some aimless transcendental reverie.

It is at this point that we shall find the Latin theological tradition helpful. That tradition never renewed its use of the image metaphor by re-sinking it into its matrix in the artwork as the Iconoclast crisis forced the Greek church to do. Instead, the Latin Church preserved the metaphor as a vehicle for teaching about man's capacity to enter into relationship with God. The theme has sound foundations among the Latin fathers, above all in Augustine's *De Trinitate*. In this work Augustine developed a subtle and profound teaching on how the soul is God's image. He discusses several psychological ternaries or trinities analogous to the divine Trinity. In Book XIV, having seen all these approaches to man's reflection of God breaking down before his eyes Augustine at last finds satisfaction in the thought that the 'trinity' of the mind is God's image not because the mind 'remembers' (or 'is present to'), understands, and loves *itself*, but because it has the power to remember, understand, and love its Maker.[8] The feeling mind, the *mens*, is only truly human when it comes to apprehend the *pulchritudo tam antiqua et tam nova*, the 'beauty at once so ancient and so new', which in the *Confessions* Augustine sees as the God present in the roots of our being.[9] Man is reformed thereby into the integral wholeness which images God.

> In sinning man lost justice and the holiness of truth; therefore, the image has become deformed and discoloured. He recovers it when he is reformed and renewed.[10]

But it was the monastic theology of the twelfth century which gave classic articulation to this teaching with a surer equilibrium, perhaps, of intellectual and affective elements than Augustine's. In writers like Bernard of Clairvaux and William of St Thierry the metaphor is set to work in an effort to show how it is by sympathetic union that man knows God. This teaching, along with its Augustinian source, influenced in its turn the presentation of the doctrine of the divine image in man in the Scholasticism of St Thomas Aquinas.[11] According to these monastic writers, it is by identification, at once affective and intellectual, with the truth disclosed in the image, Christ, that the perceiver comes to be transformed by the vision it offers.

In the theology of the twelfth-century Latin West, the theme of 'the image and likeness of God' mediates reflection on far more diverse and ramified areas of Christian faith than we are concerned with. In the words of one historian of doctrine, those two terms might serve at that epoch as 'notions crystallizing all theology'. They exercized a massively organizing influence, joining together such different theological topics and approaches as the sacramental cosmology of Hugh of St Victor in his *In hierarchiam caelestiam*;

the theology of the procession of the Holy Spirit in Richard of St Victor's *De Trinitate*; the theology of creation by the Artisan Spirit in Peter Abelard's *Introductio ad Theologiam* and other works of the Schoolmen of Chartres; the 'connections' in the ontology of the ladder of being in Abbot Isaac of Stella's *De Anima* and the spiritual theology of Bernard's *Commentary on the Song of Songs* – to name but a few. The demise of a densely symbolic theology, which had proved such a favourable setting for the theme, followed on the rise of the Aristotelean movement and provides a fairly clear *terminus ad quem* for the classic period of Latin theology of the image. In seeking a *terminus a quo*, on the other hand, we find ourselves travelling 'indefinitely far towards the sources' of the metaphor.[12] I shall consider the monastic theologians of the age in the single representative figure of *William of St Thierry*, not least because in this writer we are dealing not merely continually but continuously with material closely relevant to the theme of this chapter. For while these theologians to some extent made a fresh synthesis of general patristic teaching, their more fundamental project (nowhere clearer than in William) was to concentrate exclusively on a certain kind of question. This question was, how to precipitate the Christian listener or reader into an affective experience of his Lord in the setting of monastic fraternity and devotion. The theme of the image was invoked to release and express a sense of our movement into union, by love-knowledge, with God. Whatever the elements of the more cosmologically inclined teaching of Origen and Gregory of Nyssa on the image in man, travelling as these did by the little-known routes of baptismal catecheses and Lenten preaching on the Hexaemeron, as well as by official mediators between the two cultures such as John Scotus Erigena, the Latin monastic stress is placed resolutely on the psychological and moral aspects of the image model. Robert Javelet sees the task the monastic teachers of the age assumed as 'a psychology or descriptive phenomenology founded on an ontology of action', a striving to express the love of God at the awakening and the consummation of the creature.[13]

William's writings fall into two clusters.[14] First, there are those of his period as a black monk and abbot, finally, of the abbey of St Thierry, near Rheims. The *De contemplando Deo*, a treatise *De natura et dignitate amoris*, an anthropological essay *De natura corporis et animae* and his collected prayers, the *Meditationes orativae* are paramount here. The second grouping consists of the writings produced after 1135 when he resigned his abbacy and threw in his lot with a handful of Cistercian monks who were establishing a monastic settlement at Signy in the forest of the Ardennes. These include the *Speculum fidei* and the *Aenigma fidei* as well as the synthesis of his doctrine and experience in the *Epistola ad Fratres de Monte Dei*, more simply known as the *Golden Letter*. Connecting these two clusters is the great *Commentary on the Song of Songs*, written while William was still a Benedictine, but mulled over with his friend Bernard when both friends lay ill at Clairvaux.

In the *De natura et dignitate amoris* William opens by offering a highly Augustinian account of the divine image in man as a *memory of God* in him, a mysterious recollection of God slumbering in the depths of a person's being, a presence and living stamp of God's goodness and power.[15] Within this root possibility of experiencing the pathos of God, our destiny as creatures ordered to God is already implicit:

The memory has and holds the end towards which we are to tend; reason tells us that we must tend towards it; and the will does the tending.[16]

This *memoria* would not bring us into conscious union with God were it not for the *will* which is that stream of energy whereby we do actually tend towards God and which, under grace, becomes love. In the *De natura corporis et animae* William's Christ addresses man:

I and the Father – and my Charity – are not three but One. . . . And you, rational memory, thought and love of self, you are one man, made to the likeness of your Author, but not created his equal. For you are not begotten, you are formed, and you are not the Former. Withdraw from the things below you, less formed and less *formosa*, 'beautiful', than you. Draw near to the *Forma formatrix*, 'the formative Form', so that you may become *formosior*, 'more lovely', and cleave to it for ever. For the greater the weight of *love* that presses you against it, the deeper will be the imprint that you receive from it.[17]

143

The more a man allows himself to be moved towards God by love, the more intensely this love is illuminated until it is so penetrated by insight into God that William says you may call it 'wisdom'. It becomes a 'taste', a wholly accurate sensibility, for God. In this early treatise on the nature of Christian love, William does not suggest the character of the materials man works on in this spiritual labour. Later on, he will present them as the historical and sacramental materials of Jesus and his Church. Here he finishes by considering instead the way this transformed interior awareness he has been discussing becomes exterior and visible in us, making us into other Christs.

Their transfigured faces and bodies, their holy lives and behaviour, their mutual service and devotion, so bind each brother to his brothers that their heart and soul cannot but be one. The future glory which will be perfect in the life to come stands revealed in them already.[18]

In the *Meditationes orativae* which come from the last days of his abbacy William identifies the crucial factor in this transformation as our perception of God's 'face'. He prays:

Cause all its beams to shine upon me, that in your light I may see light. May I see how my face looks to you and yours to me, and whether just as the truth is in you, Jesus, so the truth is in me. . . .[19]

Glimpsing this face we find our own lives judged and yet at the same time, surrendering to its authority, we have the chance to break free of our egoism and live in conformity with the glorious form of God in the human:

The limits of human imperfection are never better realized than in the light of God's countenance, in the mirror which is the vision of God. Then in the light of true reality man sees more and more what he lacks and continually corrects by means of likeness whatever sins he has committed through unlikeness, drawing near by means of likeness to him from whom he has

144

been separated by unlikeness. And so clearer vision is always accompanied by a clearer likeness.[20]

William's Cistercian writings are an even richer resource of the tradition. In the *Speculum fidei* he points out that man's spirit never escapes from love of the good and the beautiful, nor from the desire for happiness. Yet if man is to apprehend adequately and concretely the good that draws him on, there must be some creative intervention of God in his world. By the twofold economy of the Son and the Holy Spirit God gives us a sacrament of himself and illuminates our spirit so that we may grasp him in it:

> Our Saviour is himself the greatest and most wonderful of the sacraments of our salvation, ordained for the forgiveness of our sins.[21]

> In the joy of enlightening grace, and in the knowledge which comes of this inward illumination, a man who hitherto could hardly call upon the Lord Jesus now cries, 'Abba, Father!' with conviction, since he is numbered among the sons of God's adoption.[22]

The charity which grace generates as the new quality of our will allows us to contemplate God in an ardour of mutual love. This love causes him to dwell in us and us to be transported into him. The personal source of grace, the Holy Spirit, dilates our love to the measure of its object for

> when we love the One who is truly to be loved, we do so under the influence of the Holy Spirit.[23]

This love-knowledge rests in what it loves, apprehended in its sign, but its rest consists of a continual 'participation and exchange'.[24] In the account of connatural knowing in this brief treatise, William sees knowledge and likeness acting in reciprocal causality:

> To be similar to God in the ultimate vision will be to see him and know him. To know him and see him will make us resemble him the more. We shall see him and know him in the same

145

proportion as we are similar to him. We shall resemble him in precisely the same measure in which we see him and know him.[25]

But the element William marks out as freeing us for this dialectical movement into God is none other than that he spoke of in his last days at St Thierry as the face of God.

We can have no true knowledge of God unless our sense of love is first conformed to the sight of God's face. Nor can our sense of love be reliable unless it makes its judgements in the light of the face of God.[26]

On the model of the artwork, we should say that it is the splendour of the divine meaning shining in the form of Christ that moves us, transforming our sensibility and habitual vision of things. Only so can we come to 'image' that face of God in Jesus by a responding love, ourselves transfigured by grace.

The fullest treatment of the theme comes, finally, in the *Commentary on the Song of Songs*, which Dom Déchanet has called 'the work, *par excellence*, of William's life'. William addresses his Lord:

O Lord our God, you did create us to your image and likeness that we might contemplate you and enjoy you. No one who contemplates you comes to enjoy you save insofar as he becomes like you. O spendour of the highest Good, you ravish with desire of you every rational soul. . . . Free then from the servitude of corruption that inner force of ours which ought to serve you alone: I mean by this our *love*.[27]

In the *Vulgate*, the Bridegroom of the Song of Songs reproaches the Bride for not being appreciative of her privilege as his lover.[28] William comments, using the grammatical first person for God:

Know yourself, then, to be my image; thus you can know me, whose image you are, and you will find me within you. . . . Seek God, therefore, in simplicity, think of him in goodness, strive to have him ever in your memory, to know him by loving him and to love him by knowing him. . . . O image of God, recognize your dignity; let the effigy of your Creator shine forth in you. To

146

yourself you seem of little worth, but in reality you are precious. . . .[29]

The Holy Spirit transforms our *desiderium tendentis*, 'the desire of the man who reaches forth' into *intellectus videntis*, 'the mind of the man who sees', and *amor fruentis*, 'the love of the man who knows joy'. Man's beauty begins to be restored by grace.

Grace, supervening, forms a man's reason and understanding, his life, manners, and even his physical temperament, into a single affection of godliness, a single *effigies* ('image') of charity, a single face – the face of one who seeks God. This man desires that the face of God's grace may be revealed to him, and that God himself may be revealed to his awareness, so that knowing him and being known by him he may pray to him and adore him as he must in spirit and in truth.[30]

In the *Preface* to the *Commentary*, in which this passage occurs, William never suggests that the disclosure of the divine face he speaks of has actually taken place, in history, in the public artwork of the Incarnate Word. But in *Stanza 7* he writes:

Created as we were to the image and likeness of the Creator, we fell through our sin from God into ourselves, and fell from ourselves beneath ourselves into such an abyss of unlikeness that no hope was left. But there came the Son of God, eternal Wisdom; he bowed the heavens and came down. He made of himself a being who should be among us and be·like us, so that we might grasp him; and he made that we be like to himself, so that we might be exalted by him. Thus the constant remembrance of this mystery would be our perpetual remedy.[31]

In perceiving God,

something comes within the grasp of the sense of enlightened love which exceeds the reach of any bodily sense, the consideration of reason, and all understanding except the understanding of enlightened love. In this state . . . there is no difference between thus grasping something of God and (by the attraction

147

of the blessed experience) becoming like to him in accord with the nature both of the impression experienced and the love that experiences it.[32]

We become 'one spirit with God, beautiful in his Beauty, good in his Goodness.'

In this theology, then, we learn to speak of a 'connatural' knowledge through which we know God by growing in his image. The creaturely process of knowledge, with its constituent elements of experience, insight and judgement, is, in its most interesting and important cases, grounded in a natural affinity of knower and known through sympathy or love.[33] An object or a person can be judged connaturally to be antipathetic, but this judgement itself presupposes a particular affinity as its basis, as when a person may be judged connaturally to be lacking in some virtue by someone who himself has an affinity with that virtue. The 'negative capability' whereby the perceiver is able to distance himself from his normal preoccupations and identify himself with the situation disclosed in the artwork is the aesthetic form of such sympathy or love. We ourselves come to 'image' the artwork. And this gives us the clue to the Latin monastic language about the image of God in man. The experience of knowing God connaturally comes about through a renewal of the divine likeness within us. That is, the deeper we move into sympathetic understanding of the artwork in its capacity to disclose the real, the more we are ourselves transformed by the vision it offers us. As the perception of meaning in the embodied form of Jesus Christ takes root in the act of faith, so it extends itself into all the reaches of our understanding and loving by assimilation to God in Christ. In the phrase of Sören Kierkegaard cited earlier, we reach out by a gesture of our whole personal subjectivity towards the Father of Jesus.

The transformation of our interior awareness and the reformation of our exterior behaviour belong together in all this. William's use of the metaphor reminds us that there is no more dichotomy between mystical awareness and ordinary Christian living than there is between the initial disclosure situation in which we see a lump of matter as an artwork and the reshaping of our existence by contemplative attention to it such as the novelists we have been looking at describe. The dimension of spiritual experience, as that is mapped by the monastic theologian, is not a purely individualistic point of contact between God and the soul somewhere on the fringe of God's revelation to mankind. Christian mystical experience is rooted intrinsically and essentially in revelation, through that judgement by connaturality in the act of faith itself.[34] William of St Thierry prefaced his Commentary on the Song of Songs by declaring that while the Lord God of all 'is to be adored and worshipped beneath the mask of many faces', yet it is the 'imaging of our embodied salvation in the Lord Jesus Christ' which alone 'passes over into love'.[35] The love in question is that distinctive charity-love of *agape*, a love which is first of all God's, disclosed in the artwork of Christ, and then secondly ours, for in learning to see into the depths of that artwork it becomes, if only after much travail and at the end, the very form of our life and sensibility.

Finally, we may close this sketch of a theology enlightened by aesthetics with a word on an objection, which, apparently imperils the thesis of this essay yet paradoxically, when viewed more profoundly, works in its favour. If the subject's response to revelation should be understood on the model of the artwork as a sympathetic interpretation of the artwork which then reshapes one's own existence – shall we not finish with as many 'revelations' as there are perceivers? As many 'aesthetic objects' as there are art-critics? The answer to this objection depends on the grasping of two vital points. Firstly, if we look to the re-creation of the image of God in actual artworks that believers have produced to show forth their sense of who Christ is, artworks sanctioned and encouraged by the Church, we have to acknowledge quite candidly that there is within the Church 'the harvest of a whole series of *Jesusbilder*'.[36] Yet there is no harm in seeing and making different pictures, for even in our common experience of human beings we do in fact apprehend different faces in one and the same person : thus the doctrine of the *epinoiai* or 'aspects' of Christ we glanced at in Origen, the multi-dimensionalism of the reality of God in Christ as that strikes and saves a diverse and multiform humanity, or even indeed one individual at different stages on life's way. Even vagueness of representation should not worry us, for we have the least stable impression of those we know best (parents, spouse, children).

But secondly, we do have a criterion for ruling out *Jesusbilder* that are simply bad, wrongheaded, and misleading, that do not

149

conform to the primordial form of the Image in objective revelation. That criterion is the New Testament witness to the Image, grasped, I have said, at the point of convergence of the interpretations offered in the various theologies accepted into the Canon. That 'point of convergence' is discovered by us not through the scientific exegesis of the texts, useful though this is, for in this case exegesis would be an inexact science, one not suited to the whole object it is to deal with. It is discovered in reading the Scriptures within the Church's living tradition: we are guided to it by the experience of the Liturgy and by the experience of the refractions of the Image in the holiness of those whom the Church raises up as saints. As Ulrich Simon has said, speaking of the contribution of the artist and the poet to our discerning of the face of God in Christ,

> We apprehend the genuine *Jesusbild* . . . not only through the achievement of genius, but also because this genius obeys the orders of Christian discipline. Hopkins' *Windhover* and *Heraclitean Fire* throw the whole Victorian concept of aesthetic beauty (which produced such a crop of maudlin images of Jesus) into the dustbin, not because Hopkins just writes good poetry, but because his *Jesusbild* rejects the false dimensions on the grounds of an ascetic, sacrificial, sacramentally ubiquitous, eternal Christ who brings resurrection not after but in death.[37]

We read the Scriptures in the Church not because of some barely masked anxiety that the acid of scientific criticism will corrode the image of Christ into a meaningless blur, but because in the living stream of the Church's experience we find an interpretative medium for the Scriptures which plays something of the same role in evaluating them as does a critical tradition in bringing to bear an appropriate sensibility and judgement on secular literature. The Bible, after all, was written by the Church and for the Church. It is not a source-book for faith, to be quarried by whatever textual or philosophical tools may be to hand, but a living fountain of truth for the man or woman of the Church who has already received the faith. I single out for particular mention here the relevance of sacramental experience and of acquaintance with the Christian saints as crucial cues in seeking the authentic image of Christ in the New Testament. This is because in the Liturgy and in the saints

150

the Church is supremely herself as the community which lives by rapport with Jesus, contemplating him, in communion with him.

Resurrexi et adhuc tecum sum. 'I am risen, and am still with you.' I take this to imply that the deepest insights into the meaning of Jesus are to be found in the faith of the Church where he is present in word and sacrament. . . . We do not simply examine Jesus historically to see what he was like; we listen to him, he established communication and friendship with us, and it is in this rapport with Jesus that we explore a different dimension of his existence. . . .[38]

It is this ecclesial dimension which is needed to complement and complete Etienne Trocmé's account in his excellent study of the historical Jesus, where he expresses his refusal to choose between 'the very different portraits of the person and work of Jesus that we find in the pre-gospel tradition'. The diversity of that tradition, Trocmé shows, derives from the encounter of Jesus with 'groups who were as different from each other as they could be'. Trocmé goes on,

Nothing said or done in the sight of any of the groups whom Jesus encountered would have had much significance if he had not been marvelled at by those with whom he came into contact. Thus the portrait of the Master found in the tradition which derives from different groups reflects this unbreakable union between the work and its author. By accepting it in each case, Jesus showed that he had claimed a very high authority, the highest that the group was prepared to accord him. By not proposing a synthesis between these portraits, he suggested that none of them, and none of those which could be superimposed upon them, could do full justice to his person and his mission. Thus the 'mystery of Jesus' is not a more or less artificial creation by later generations. It is rooted in the behaviour of Jesus himself, completely devoted to his humble task, but convinced that for this mission he possessed an exceptional authority from God; involved in several simultaneous dialogues and not trying to draw them into a unity; too great to be wholly understood by any of his interloctutors, but grasped in part by many of them.

151

This mystery already necessitated the groping efforts of the evangelists and theologians of the first century. It has never been finally eliminated, either by historians or by theologians. It never will be.[39]

Appendix: On Models and Metaphors

The human thirst to find analogies, intelligible links and consonances, between various aspects of experience, and various faces of the cosmos seems as deep as the well of the past. In ancient Greek thought before Plato, argument in terms of analogy enjoyed a wide currency, because (it has been said) it carried the accolade of 'the success with which the first philosophers and scientists adapted analogies to express conceptions of the cosmos as a whole and to suggest accounts of obscure natural phenomena'.[1] The roots of analogical apprehension, however, lie in the very character of human language itself, as a symbolizing instrument. Distinctively human communication lies in man's power to give and receive signs not just as stimuli to behavioural and emotive responses but also as symbols – as representing something for its own sake. The creative and discriminating activity of language-users confers on these symbols a capacity to take on new reference – to speak of one order in terms of another, usually a more familiar, realm of experience.[2] The modern student of the ancient and endemic pursuit of analogy prefers to speak of models, metaphors and paradigms – and in so doing he has the virtue of sorting out for us rather different types of transferred language.

According to a recent and reliable exposé, a model may be defined as 'a symbolic representation of selected aspects of the behaviour of a complex system for particular purposes'.[3] The definition sounds alarmingly likely to belong to a study of the national economy or the behaviour of sub-atomic particles, rather than to reflection on the disclosure of the God of Christian faith: yet all three of these subject-matters at least have it in common that they cannot be represented in wholly adequate concepts – they escape a neat, univocal and once-for-all grid of ideas which we would place over them. The use of models in theology is implicit, it might be said, in

153

the very texture of the Scriptures of the Old and New Testaments, since these work with great organizing images, by a 'glass of vision'.[4] But there is a difference easier perhaps to sense than to state between a metaphor and a model. We shall return to this in a moment. For the present it may suffice to say that the explicit use of models in systematic theology derives from the transferral to reflection on God of an approach whose original home lies with the natural sciences. Theoretical models in science originate in a combination of analogy to the familiar, and creative imagination in the invention of the new. Such models in, say, physics are not simply labour-saving devices, a kind of shorthand to save the student of ultimate particles of matter from premature seizures of the brain. They have been found to have a genuine heuristic value – that is, they enable scientists (and philosophers of science too) to raise interesting and important questions about the reality the student is concerned with via the model.[5] The model of the billiard-ball in the kinetic theory of gases, for example, continues to suggest modifications in existing theory and the discovery of new phenomena.[6] Such models are 'taken seriously but not literally'. They are neither literal pictures of reality nor useful fictions, belief-systems which fulfil important functions within a mental culture but are not used to make assertions about what is the case. Models are, it seems, partial, provisional ways of imagining what is not observable; they are symbolic representations of aspects of the world which are not directly accessible to us.

The model has two uses therefore. Firstly, it gives vividness or immediacy to a theory by offering as an interpretation of the abstract or unfamiliar theory structure something that both fits the logical form of the theory and is well-known. Secondly, it contributes to a more inclusive account of experience by its power to relate some single theory plausibly to our whole account of reality, linking widely divergent domains of understanding in a freshly intelligible way.

The suggested model in this essay has been the model of the artwork in the theology of revelation. In Britain anyhow the main source of interest to students of the application of models to Christian faith has been religious language, the direct language of religious faith, rather than theology. It is wise to keep the two kinds of language nicely distinct, and that implies that we shall find rather different uses for the theory of models, as we look now to the one, now to the other. It might perhaps be possible to assert of a theological model, as has been said of a model implicit in the language of the Bible, that it is applied in order to 'interpret distinctive types of experience', citing among these the experience of awe, of moral obligation, of conversion and reconciliation, of key historical events, of order and creativity in the world.[7] But it would seem clearer and more accurate to separate out two levels in the interpretation of such experiences – if we allow that this list or a list more inclusive but of the same sort does direct our attention to the founding experiences of Christianity. At one level there are the models used in the Scriptures where these experiences have their primary witness – for instance the model of fatherhood in Jesus' teaching about God. At a second level, there are models used in ordering the theological resources suggested by the complex of models (and metaphors) in the Scriptures. It is at this second level that the present essay has moved, although it is inevitable that reference must be made via the first level of the scriptural models to the 'creative rupture' in experience which generated the distinctive insights of Christianity.

A second difference between models in religious language and in theology is that, although theology is indeed concerned with the movement of the mind-in-love towards God, it entertains this concern in its own proper way, the way that belongs to theological science as such. The imagery of theological models is not directly concerned to elicit self-commitment to the ultimate values discerned in the life-way of Christianity. The theological model does not in any obvious sense, unlike the model in the first-order language of faith, worship, and prayer, express or evoke distinctive attitudes – except, of course, the attitude of growing or decreasing conviction of its usefulness in ordering the materials of theology!

We may now turn to a brief consideration of metaphor in theology. To utter a metaphor is to propose an analogy between the normal context of a word and a new context in which it is introduced. Some of the familiar associations of a word are transferred to serve as a screen or lens through which a new subject is viewed. Two frames of reference are juxtaposed. There is, in the critic I. A. Richards' phrase, 'a transaction between contexts'.[8] To grasp the metaphor is to apprehend the meaning which stands at the intersection of two perspectives; to explore the metaphor is to maintain an awareness of both the contexts, allowing them to illuminate each other in unexpected ways. It is this last feature of metaphorical language which ensures that it is not, even in principle, reducible to literal statements – metaphor has an unspecifiable number of potentialities latent within it. This may remind us of the way the scientific model is of more than merely psychological value, since it is based on analogies which are 'open-ended' and extensible. Unlike scientific models, and unlike theological models, too, but much closer to models in religious language, metaphors aim to call forth feelings and attitudes as well as to shape perception and interpretation. They are emotional, evaluative, and cognitive, all at the same time. A poem, even though it may make only 'a shy ontological claim'[9] has, as a verbal icon of metaphors, a cognitive side which is the heart of our concern here – for no essay about revelation will serve unless it shows how revelation gives access to what really is. Metaphor says something, however tentatively and obliquely, about the nature of things.

One way of stating the relationship between a metaphor and a model is to say that models are metaphors when systematically developed. Metaphors occur as momentary occasions in poetic language; models organize, restructure selectively and re-interpret our perceptions, pervading an intellectual tradition by their presence. But presumably not all metaphors are capable of transforming themselves into models: so how is the choice made? How do we know which associations of the original metaphor, furthermore, yield the aspects of the model that we must pursue, the really isomorphic features of the two realities we have before us? And does that word 'systematic' adequately distinguish the way a literary critic probes the meanings of a metaphor from the work of the theologian applying his model?[10]

These are questions on which the author of this book would be glad of further enlightenment. They are posed here to indicate his awareness of the unfinished character of his proposals.

Metaphors and models give access to the real, and they are vital and indispensable when it is the mysterious, many-sided simplicities of man and God we have to talk about. So much is clear enough. This book has tried to show how an original metaphor, created by the Priests in the Exile, has generated a 'theology of the painterly image' in Christian tradition. It has aimed at demonstrating how the model implicit in that theology can be turned to good use today in giving an account of how revelation happens in Christ – drawing on our experience of the better known, namely art, to illuminate the less well known, namely God in Christ. It seems important to say, however, that it is unlikely that catholic theology will be satisfied with the currently dominant view of models in English philosophy of religion, that of the late Ian Ramsey.[11] By making models tools for the evocation of 'disclosure situations' in our experience, Ramsey bypasses the problem of their relation to each other and to anything outside man. Yet surely we need to show the coherence and consistency of the different models we use in any given domain of theology. One criterion for selecting those aspects of a model likely to give veridical insights into the reality of God will be a criterion of compatibility with the meanings given in other images and concepts which have achieved a key interpretative place in church tradition. Some of these, such as the concept of nature in the teaching of Chalcedon make bold and direct ontological claims, while others, such as the various biblical images for the Atonement, offer a 'shyer' claim. A Christian ontology of the experience of faith and grace – that is, an account of the shape of reality as disclosed in that experience – will come to birth if duly nourished by the resources of meaning given in all of these. At the same time, its makers will have to attend to the demands of coherence among them, and those of correspondence and compatibility with what we know to be the case through secular experience.

Notes

Preface

1 Cited in E. Gilson, *The Mystical Theology of St Bernard* (London 1940), p. 77.
2 Julian of Norwich, *Revelations of Divine Love*, 27, ed. G. Warrack (London 1901), p. 56.
3 See J. Coulson, *Newman and the Common Tradition* (Oxford 1970), ch. 1, 'Coleridge, Bentham and the fiduciary use of language'.
4 J. Hick, ed., *The Myth of God Incarnate* (London 1977).
5 See Hick, ed., op. cit., p. 4, where Maurice Wiles is the questioner in his essay 'Christianity without Incarnation?'

Chapter 1: Setting the Scene

1 See for instance A. Smith, *The Shadow in the Cave* (London 1973); The Glasgow University Media Group, *Bad News* (London 1976).
2 A. Malraux, *The Museum without Walls* (London 1967).
3 R. Huyghe, *The Discovery of Art* (London 1959), ch. 1.
4 G. Steiner, *Language and Silence* (abridged edn, Harmondsworth 1969), p. 13.
5 Addison in *The Spectator* No. 416, for 1712, cited by H. Osborne, *Aesthetics and Art Theory* (London and Harlow 1968), p. 97.
6 Vasari, *Lives of the Artists*, tr. G. de Vere (London 1912-15), I, p. 136.
7 E. Auerbach, *Mimesis* (Princeton 1953), *passim*.
8 N. Scott, *The Wild Prayer of Longing* (New Haven 1971).
9 T. S. Eliot, 'The Burial of the Dead', *The Waste Land*, I, in *Collected Poems* (London 1936).
10 P. Pool, *Impressionism* (London 1967), pp. 12-15. See also L. Venturi, *Archives de l'Impressionisme* (Paris and New York 1939) for Pissarro's letter of 6 November 1886 to Durand-Ruel.
11 The combination is found in J. M. W. Turner. See J. Lindsay, *Turner* (London 1966), pp. 273-82.
12 W. C. Seitz, *Claude Monet* (London 1960).
13 P. Pool, op. cit., p. 91.
14 A. C. Bridge, *Images of God* (London 1960), p. 98.
15 B. H. Steinberg, *Understanding Gauguin* (London 1976), p. 28.
16 A. J. Lubin, *Stranger on the Earth: the Life of Vincent van Gogh* (St

Albans 1975), pp. 271-3.

Chapter 2: The Images of Israel

1 On this see U. Mauser, *Gottesbild und Menschwerdung* (Tübingen 1971).
2 This is Mauser's solution to the problem of the relation between the Testaments central to 'Biblical Theology'.
3 Johannes Pedersen, a moderate Danish member of this School, wrote that 'All the sources of the Pentateuch are both pre-exilic and post-exilic', 'Die Auffassung vom Alten Testament', *Zeitschrift für die Alttestamentliche Wissenschaft* XXXXIX (1931), pp. 161–81.
4 G. von Rad, *Genesis* (3rd edn, London 1972), pp. 27-8.
5 R. E. Clements, *God and Temple* (Oxford 1965), pp. 100-23.
6 Gen. 9.6.
7 See James Barr, 'The Image of God in the Book of Genesis: A Study of Terminology', *BJRL* LI (1968-9).
8 Gen. 1. 26-8.
9 Von Rad detects this red herring in his commentary on Genesis, where he is also clear that the theme of man's dominion in the passage belongs not so much to the definition of the image as to its implications.
10 See D. Cairns, *The Image of God in Man* (revised edn, London 1973).
11 P. Humbert, *Études sur le récit du paradis et de la chute dans la Génèse* (Neuchâtel 1940), pp. 151-75.
12 J. Hehn, 'Zum Terminus "Bild Gottes"', *Festschrift Eduard Sachau* (Berlin 1918), pp. 36-52.
13 This account draws on H. Ringgren, *Religions of the Ancient Near East* (London 1973).
14 W. G. Lambert, 'The Great Battle of the Mesopotamian Religious Year: the Conflict in the Akitu House', *Iraq* (1963), pp. 189f, cited in Ringgren, op. cit.
15 See P. Humbert, 'La relation de Génèse 1 et du ps. 104 avec la liturgie du nouvel An israélite', *Revue d'histoire et de philosophie religieuse* (1935). A good account of the probable influence of the New Year festival on the life of Israel may be found in J. H. Eaton, *Kingship and the Psalms* (London 1976).
16 G. van der Leuuw, *Religion in Essence and Manifestation* (London 1938), pp. 447-8.
17 G. van der Leuuw, *Sacred and Profane Beauty* (London 1963), pp. 306-7.
18 J. Barr, art. cit.
19 Isa. 40.25.
20 Ps. 135.15; Isa. 44; Wisd.13.10-19; Letter of Jeremiah h Baruch 6.
21 Satires I. 8,1.
22 E. Bevan, *Holy Images* (London 1940), p. 38.
23 Judg. 8.27.

24 Judg.17.
25 H. Thiersch, *Ependytes und Ephod: Gottesbild und Priesterkleid im alten Vorasien* (Stuttgart 1936), p. 120, cited in W. F. Albright, *Yahweh and the Gods of Canaan* (London 1968).
26 Gen. 31. 10-21, 31–5.
27 Deut. 27, 11–26. See G. von Rad, *Old Testament Theology* (Edinburgh 1962), I, p. 215.
28 Ib, p. 216.
29 Deut. 4.12.
30 G. von Rad, op.cit., p. 217.
31 Exod. 20.21.
32 V. Lossky, 'The Theology of the Image', *Sob.* 3,22 (1957-8), p. 515. See also his *In the Image and Likeness of God* (New York 1974), p. 133.
33 A. J. Heschel, *The Prophets* (New York 1962), II, *passim*.
34 Ib., p. 9.
35 Isa. 20.
36 The parables in the story of Jeremiah include the Almond Tree and the Pot, 1.11–14; the Hidden Loincloth, 13.1–11; the Potter, 18.1–12; the Jug, 19; the Figs, 24; the Yoke, 27–8; the Buying of the Field, 32. In the life of Ezekiel we find the Besieged Brick, 4.1–3; the Ration of Food, 4. 9–17; the Hair, 5; the Mime of the Exile, 12. 1–20; the Pot, 24.3–14; the Two Sticks, 37.15–28.
37 U. Mauser, op. cit., p. 17.
38 J. Hempel, *Das Ethos des Alten Testaments* (Berlin 1938), p. 198.
39 H. Wheeler Robinson, 'The Cross of Hosea' in *Two Hebrew Prophets: Studies in Hosea and Ezekiel* (London 1948).
40 Hos. 2.19–20.
41 Jer. 20. 14–18 where the curse on the prophet's pre-natal existence is really an accusation against God for shaping Jeremiah to his destiny.
42 Jer. 1.18.
43 Compare Jer. 20.9 with Isa. 50.5, and Jer. 11.19 with Isa. 53.7. Jeremiah like the Isaianic Servant is free from the people's guilt yet remains identified with them, in the prophet's case by staying in Jerusalem after the city's fall.
44 H. Mauser, op. cit., p. 110.
45 S. Kierkegaard, *The Present Age* (London 1940), pp. 139-63.

Chapter 3: Christ, the Image of God

1   The most recent discussion, that of E. P. Sanders, *Paul and Palestinian Judaism* (London 1977), insists that Paul grounds his theology on the meaning of the death and resurrection of Jesus rather than fitting 'the death and resurrection into a pre-existing scheme, where they take the place of other motifs with similar functions', p. 556. Yet Sanders' book is itself a massive testimony to Paul's indebtedness to the language and

concepts of Palestinian (and to a lesser degree, Hellenistic) Judaism.

2 G. F. Moore, *Judaism* (Cambridge, Massachusetts, 1927), I, p. 479.
3 *Genesis Rabba* 24 on Gen. 5.1. This and cognate rabbinic testimonies are gathered conveniently in G. Kittel, G. von Rad, and H. Kleinknecht, 'Eikon' in Kittel, ed., *Theological Dictionary of the New Testament*, II (Grand Rapids 1964).
4 J. Jervell, *Imago Dei* (Göttingen 1960), p. 114.
5 R. Scroggs, *The Last Adam* (Oxford 1966) pp. 52–4.
6 Ib., pp. 23–31; 54–8.
7 Ib., p. 24. Writers here would include the author of the *Apocalypse of Moses* and of 1 Enoch: these texts may be found in R. H. Charles, *The Apocrypha and Pseudepigrapha of the Old Testament* (Oxford 1913). Scroggs has brought together a number of pertinent rabbinic texts. He writes:

'The prior concept is the eschatological glory. The theologians are not seriously concerned about Adam as a mythic personality but rather about the eschatological future of Israel. Adam is invested with the glory of the saints because the new man can only be the recreation of what truly existed in the *Urzeit*' (op.cit., p. 27).

8 *Baba Bathra* 58a and *Baba Metzia* 84a. These texts may be found in I. Epstein, *The Babylonian Talmud* (London 1935–52) See R. Scroggs, op.cit., p.45.
9 *Apocalypse of Moses* 39.2.
10 Wisd. 7.26.
11 G. von Rad, *Wisdom in Israel* (London 1972), pp. 144-76.
12 P. Brown, 'Eastern and Western Christianity in Late Antiquity: A Parting of the Ways', in *The Orthodox Churches and the West* (Studies in Church History, Vol. xiii), ed. D. Baker (Oxford 1976), pp. 1–24.
13 E. R. Goodenough, *Jewish Symbols in the Greco-Roman Period* (New York 1953-65), I, pp. 181-92, 199-225. Also E. L. Sukenik, *Ancient Synagogues in Palestine and Greece* (London 1932).
14 E. Goodenough, op.cit., II, pp. 4–44.
15 Ib, I, 227–32. Also M. Rostovtzeff, *Dura-Europos and its Art* (Oxford 1938), and on the orthodoxy of this community see A. Perkins, *The Art of Dura-Europos* (Oxford 1973).
16 E. R. Goodenough, op.cit., III, p.50. The Zechariah text is 4.2f.
17 Morton Smith, 'The Image of God : notes on the hellenisation of Judaism with especial reference to Goodenough's work on Jewish symbols', *BJRL* XL (1958), pp. 473–512.
18 J. B. Frey, 'La question des images chez les juifs à la lumière des récentes découvertes', *Biblica* XV (1934), pp. 265–300.
19 Morton Smith, art. cit.
20 Acts 16.6, 18.23.
21 This account follows closely that of J. H. Houlden, *Paul's Letters from Prison* (Harmondsworth 1970).
22 E. W. Burton, *The Epistle to the Galatians* (Edinburgh 1921), p. 189.

23 Romans 8.2.
24 E. Bammel, 'Versuch zu Kol.1, 15–20', *Zeitschrift für die Neutesta-mentliche Wissenschaft* (1961), pp. 881f.
25 C. F. Burney, 'Christ as the *ARXH* of the Creation', *JTS* 27 (1926), pp. 106ff.
26 Ib.
27 C. K. Barrett, *From First Adam to Last* (London 1962), pp. 3–4.
28 See F. F. Bruce, *Paul and Jesus* (Grand Rapids 1974), p. 52.
29 1 Cor. 2.16.
30 For an application of the thought of H. G. Gadamer on hermeneutical distance to the New Testament, see Franz Mussner, *The Historical Jesus in the Gospel of John* (London 1967).
31 G. Bornkamm, *Paul* (London 1971), pp. xxiv–xxv.
32 1 Cor. 15.44b–49.
33 R. Scroggs, op.cit. p. 93.
34 *Genesis Rabba* xiv. 5, in *Midrash Rabbah* (Vilna 1887)
35 Degas' words cited by M. Levey, *A Concise History of Painting from Giotto to Cézanne* (London 1962), p. 296.
36 Phil. 2.6–11 on which see R. P. Martin, *Carmen Christi* (Cambridge 1967).
37 See Chapter 7.
38 See Chapter 8.
39 This discussion of 2 Corinthians 3–4 is much indebted to C. K. Barrett, *A Commentary on the Second Epistle to the Corinthians* (London 1973).
40 C. K. Barrett, *From First Adam to Last*, op.cit., p. 99.
41 2 Cor. 3.12–18.
42 A. Feuillet, *Le Christ, Sagesse de Dieu, d'après les épitres pauliniennes* (Paris 1960).
43 Philo Judaeus, *Legum allegoriae* III, 101.
44 Outside of Romans 12, this is Paul's only use of this striking verb. Taken together with such other terms as *photismos, phos, elampsen,* and *prosopon* it suggests an acquaintance with the Marcan account of Jesus' transfiguration or something very like it. Perhaps Paul begins here from Synoptic (or Synoptic-type) material which he then turns into direct teaching by way of the midrash on Exodus.
45 2 Cor. 4.1–6.
46 C. K. Barrett, *A Commentary on the Second Epistle to the Corinthians,* op.cit., p. 126.
47 Ib., p. 141. See also C. K. Barrett, *The Signs of an Apostle* (London 1970).
48 A. T. Hanson, *Grace and Truth,* op.cit., ch. 1, 'Jesus Christ as grace and truth'.
49 The Johannine structure is (a) the revelation of the divine Name consisting in the disclosure of God as wholly faithful love; (b) this revelation mediated by the Son's obedience to his Father in his incarnate love;

(c) and manifested to the world by the mutual love and service of the members of the Church. The pattern is most sharply focused in the Last Supper Discourse.

50 In the Letter to the Hebrews the divine image is mediated by the Son's 'learning obedience through what he suffered', 5.8.

Chapter 4: The Art of God in the World of the Fathers

1 John 4.24.

2 Synagogue art had not yet been uncovered. Yet texts were at hand to show that the interpretation of the status and meaning of the Ten Commandments was no clear-cut affair in the early Church. See below, n. 4.

3 Clement, *Stromateis* VI. 133–48. *GCS* II.499, 12–508, 20.

4 R. M. Grant, 'The Decalogue in Early Christianity', *HThR* XL (1947), pp. 1–17.

5 Sister Charles Murray, S.N.D., 'Art and the Early Church', *JTS* (October 1977).

6 E. Renan, *Histoire des Origines du Christianisme* (Paris 1863–83), VII, 'Marc Aurèle et la Fin du Monde Antique'.

7 B. F. Westcott, 'The relation of Christianity to Art', reprinted in *The Epistles of St John* (Cambridge 1886), pp. 317–60.

8 B. F. Westcott, op. cit, pp. 325–6.

9 Ib., p. 348.

10 Evidence for their official character is available in Hippolytus. See *Traditio Apostolica* XXX in B. Botte, *Hippolyte de Rome, La Tradition Apostolique*, *SC* 11 (Paris 1946); and *Philosophumena* IX.12, 14 in J. Legge, *Philosophumena* (London 1921).

11 Giovanni Battista de Rossi directed the Roman archaeologists who worked on the catacombs from 1830 onwards. His approach is at least partially vindicated in A. Grabar, *Christian Iconography* (London 1969).

12 A fresco in Chamber A2, the oldest part of the Catacomb of St Callistus, dated to c. 200 A.D.

13 Now in the inner courtyard of the Lateran Museum but originally a find from the Roman cemeteries.

14 F. van der Meer, *Early Christian Art* (London 1967), pp. 92, 96.1

15 E. Kitzinger, 'The Cult of the Image before Iconoclasm', *DOP* VIII (1954).

16 Asterius of Amasea, *Homilia* 11, *In laudem sancti Stephani*. PG 40, 337BC.

17 Hypatius' letter to Julian of Atramytion was published by F. Diekamp in 'Analecta Patristica', *Orientalia Christiana Analecta* CXVII (Rome 1938). See P. J. Alexander, 'Hypatius of Ephesus: A note on image worship in the sixth century', *HThR* (1952).

18 E.g. John Moschus, *Pratum Spirituale*, 180. PG 87-3. 3057AC.

19 *Sancti Maximi Confessoris Acta* II, 16 and 26; PG 90, 156AB and 164 AB.
20 See P. Brown, 'A Dark-Age Crisis: aspects of the Iconoclastic Controversy', *English Historical Review* CCCXLVI (January 1973), pp. 1–34.
21 Ib., pp. 10–12.
22 Ib., p. 15.
23 Gregory of Nyssa, *Encomium on Theodore the Martyr*. PG 46, 740.
24 Sr C. Murray, S.N.D., art.cit. The texts may be found in H. Hennephof, *Textus byzantinis ad Iconomachiam pertinentes* (Leipzig 1969).
25 His phrase is *graphe sioposa*.
26 Paulinus of Nola, *De sancti Felici natalitio carmen* IX.541ff. PL 61, 660C–661A.
27 Gregory the Great, *The Book of Letters* IX.105. PL 77, 1027CD–1028A; XI.13. PL 77, 1128A–1130B.
28 Gregory of Nyssa, *Oratio de deitate Filii et Spiritus Sancti*. PG 46, 572C.
29 Philostorgus, *Historia ecclesiastica* VII.3. PG 65, 540.
30 Ps-Athanasius, *Quaestiones ad Antiochum ducem* 39. PG 28, 621B.
31 Denys' teaching is summarized conveniently in I. P. Sheldon-Williams, 'The Greek Christian Platonist Tradition from the Cappadocians to Maximus and Eriugena' in A. H. Armstrong, ed., *The Cambridge History of Later Greek and Early Mediaeval Philosophy* (Cambridge 1967), pp. 457–72. Sheldon-Williams traces Denys' influence on the 'philosophy of icons' on pp. 506–9.
32 Hypatius of Ephesus, *The Miscellaneous Enquiries*. See above, n. 17.
33 N. H. Baynes, 'The Icons before Iconoclasm' in *Byzantine Studies and Other Essays* (London 1955).
34 John Damascene, *On the Holy Images*. PG 94, 1232A–1429C.
35 Leontius, *Sermo contra Judaeos*. PG 93, 1604CD.
36 George Pisides, *De expeditione persica* I, 145. PG 92, 1208A.
37 See E. von Dobschütz, *Christusbilder* (2nd edn, Leipzig 1909), pp. 12f.
38 J. D. Mansi, *Sacrorum Conciliorum nova et amplissima collectio* (Florence 1758–98), XI, pp. 977f.
39 For instance, H. Crouzel, S. J., *Théologie de l'image de Dieu chez Origène* (Paris 1956); R. Leys, *L'Image de Dieu chez S. Grégoire de Nysse* (Paris 1951); R. Bernard, *L'image de Dieu chez S. Athanase* (Paris 1952); A. Mayer, *Das Bild Gottes im Menschen nach Clemens von Alexandrien* (Rome 1942); W. Burghardt, *The Image of God in Man according to Cyril of Alexandria* (Washington 1957).
40 G. B. Ladner, 'The concept of the image in the Greek Fathers and the Byzantine Iconoclastic Controversy', *DOP* VII (1953).
41 'Irenaeus' in F. D. Cross and E. A. Livingstone, ed., *The Oxford Dictionary of the Christian Church* (2nd edn, London 1974).
42 J. Lawson, *The Biblical Theology of St Irenaeus* (London 1948).
43 See H. Jonas, *The Gnostic Religion* (Boston 1958).
44 Irenaeus, *Contra Haereses* I. 5,5. PG 7, 500B-501A.

45 Ib., V. 6, 1. PG 7, 1137A.
46 Ib., V. 16,2. PG 7, 1167C–1168A.
47 Ib., and also IV. 33, 4. PG 7, 1057AB. See too J. A. Robinson, ed., *St Irenaeus, The Demonstration of the Apostolic Preaching* (London 1920), ch. 22.
48 Irenaeus, *Contra Haereses* IV. 34, 1.PG 7, 1083C.
49 H. Chadwick, *Early Christian Thought and the Classical Tradition* (Oxford 1966).
50 Clement, *Stromateis* V. 16 5; GCS II. 336, 12–14.
51 Clement, *Protreptikos*, 113,3, GCS 1.79, 30–80, 25.
52 Clement, *Stromateis* V. 38,6., GCS II. 352, 13–17
53 A. Grillmeier, S. J., *Christ in Christian Tradition* (1st edn, London 1965), pp. 162–3).
54 C. von Schönborn, O. P., *L'Icône du Christ* (Fribourg 1976), p. 78; G. Florovsky, 'Origen, Eusebius and the Iconoclastic Controversy', *ChH* 19 (1950).
55 Origen, *De Principiis* II. 6,3. GCS V. 142, 5–15.
56 M. Harl, *Origène et la fonction révélatrice du Verbe incarné* (Paris 1958), pp. 191–200.
57 H. de Lubac, S. J., *Histoire et Esprit: L'Intelligence de l'Ecriture d'après Origène* (Paris 1950). Père de Lubac, although anxious to make the best case possible for Origen's theological balance, found himself obliged to write, 'Tied to the mystery of the Incarnation, if history is indeed mediatory, still, it must not hold us back. On the contrary its entire task is to *pass*' (p. 282 his stress).
58 Origen, *Contra Celsum* 4,31; GCS II.301. 3,76; GCS ii.268.
59 A. Grillmeier, op.cit., p. 164.
60 Ib. p. 168.
61 Origen, *Commentary on the Gospel of John* X.5 (4), 21. PG 14, 313B–316C; See A. Orbe, S. J., *La Epinoia* (Rome 1955), pp 26–32, and F. Bertrand, *Mystique de Jésus chez Origène* (Paris 1951), pp. 15–46.
62 See below, chapter 9.
63 Hennephof, op.cit., No. 242, p. 272. PG 20, 1545A–1548A. J. Boivin and Cardinal Pitra assembled the text from a passage in the Iconoclastic *Florilegium* of 754. Its authenticity has been questioned by Sr C. Murray, art. cit. Yet there seems small likelihood that apologists would fabricate the texts of a theologian not fully orthodox by later criteria.
64 C. von Schönborn, op.cit., pp. 58–62.
65 E.g. Eusebius, *Demonstratio evangelica* V. 8; GCS VI, p. 230, 19–30.
66 Ib., IV.2,2; GCS VI. p. 152, 8–14; IV. 4,2; GCS VI, p. 155, 2; V. 13,4; GCS VI, p. 171, 25–7.
67 C. von Schönborn, op.cit., p. 68.
68 Eusebius, *Theophania* (Greek fragments) 3; GCS III, p. 4, 12.
69 Eusebius, *Praeparatio evangelica* III. 10,15–17; GCS VIII, p. 133, 8.20.

70 Eusebius, *Historia ecclesiastica* VII. 18,4; *GCS* II, p. 673.

71 Eusebius, *Letter to Constantia*, PG 20, 1548D–9A.

72 Basil, *Letter* 38. PG 32,235A–341B. R. Hübner has suggested recently that the letter may really be by Gregory of Nyssa: 'Gregor von Nyssa als Verfasser der sogenannten Ep. 38 des Basilius', in J. Fontaine and Ch. Kanengiesser, ed., *Epektasis. Mélanges patristiques offerts au Card. J. Daniélou* (Paris 1972).

73 Hebrews 1.3.

74 Basil, op.cit.

75 C. von Schönborn, op.cit., p. 42.

76 Basil, *De Spiritu Sancto* 18,45. PG 32, 145.

77 Gregory of Nyssa, *Homilia in diem natalem Christi*. PG 46, 7141B.

78 Gregory of Nyssa, *Contra Eunomium* II, 215–6. PG 45, 891D–984A.

79 M. de Durand, O.P., ed., *Cyrille d'Alexandrie, Deux dialogues christologiques SC* 97 (Paris 1964).

80 Cyril, *Quod unus sit Christus*. PG 75, 1329A.

81 Ib.

82 Cyril, *Scholia de incarnatione Unigeniti*. PG 75, 1379D–1382B.

83 Cyril, *Quod unus sit Christus*. PG 75, 1361A.

84 Ib. PG 75, 1288C.

85 Ps. 20.10.

86 Cyril, *Glossa in Genesim* III. 8.PG 69, 132AB.

87 Cyril, *In Joannem* 14.9. PG 74, 209D–212A.

88 E. von Dobschütz, op.cit., p. 33.

89 Cyril, *Letter to the Monks for Easter 429*. PG 77, 32B.

90 C. von Schonborn, op.cit., p. 103. Compare Cyril, *In Joannem* 1,32–3. PG 73,204D, and *Thesaurus*, Assertio XIII, PG 75, 228B.

91 M. J. Le Guillou, O.P., in his introduction to J. M. Garrigues, O. P., *Maxime le Confesseur. La charité avenir divin de l'homme* (Paris 1974).

92 Maximus, *Disputatio cum Pyrrho*. PG 91, 304C.

93 Maximus, *Opera theologica et polemica* 16. PG 91, 193A.

94 Maximus, *Letter* 2. PG 91, 397A.

95 Maximus, *Liber asceticus* 13. PG 90, 921BC.

96 Maximus, *Letter* 44. PG 91, 644B.

97 A. Riou, O.P. *Le monde et l'église selon Maxime le Confesseur* (Paris 1973), pp. 111–12, commenting on Maximus, *Ambigua* 10, 31. PG 91, 1165D–1168A.

Chapter 5: The Vindication of the Icons

1 J. Pelikan, *The Spirit of Eastern Christendom* (Chicago 1974), p. 92.

2 P. Henry, 'What was the Iconoclast Controversy About?' *ChH* XLV (1976), pp. 16–31.

3 See Chapter 4.

4 G. Ostrogorsky, *History of the Byzantine State* (Oxford 1956), p. 143.

5   Ib., pp. 142–3.
6   C. de Boor, ed., *Theophanes, Chronographia* (Leipzig 1883–5), p. 401.
7   P. Brown, 'A Dark-Age Crisis. . . .', art. cit.
8   Germanus, *De haeresibus et synodis*. PG 98, 80.
9   G. Ostrogorsky, op.cit., p. 152.
10 The texts are collected in G. Ostrogorsky, *Studien der Geschichte des byzantinischen Bilderstreits* (Breslau 1929), pp. 8f.
11 C. Mango, 'Historical Introduction' in A. Bryer and J. Herrin, ed., *Iconoclasm* (Birmingham 1975), p. 3.
12 J. D. Mansi, op.cit., XIII. 225.
13 Theodore of Studios, *Refutatio poematum iconomachorum*. PG 99, 437C; 461B–5A.
14 J.-D. Mansi, op. cit., XIII. 345.
15 Constantine's teaching has been transmitted in fragments embedded in the *Antirrhetica* of Nicephorus of Constantinople. PG 100, 205A–533A. We take up the text at 260C–1A and 264D.
16 S. Brock, 'Iconoclasm and the Monophysites' in A. Bryer and J. Herrin, *Iconoclasm*, op.cit.
17 J.-D.Mansi, op.cit., XIII. 256f.
18 P. Henry, art.cit.
19 C. Mango, art.cit., p. 4.
20 Stephen the Deacon, *Life of St Stephen the Younger*. PG 100, 1117–1160.
21 J.-D.Mansi, op.cit., XIII.352.
22 This summary of events is largely indebted to those of Ostrogorsky and Mango cited above.
23 The Office for the Sunday of Orthodoxy in the Byzantine Rite combines a reference to the theo-political element in the struggle over the icons with an affirmation of the portrayable quality of the Word Incarnate. The liturgy appropriates Ps. 92.1 'The Lord is King, and has put on glorious apparel'.
24 Theophanes, op.cit., ad annum 6221, ed. de Boor, p. 407.
25 Germanus, *Letter to John of Synades*, cited in Mansi XIII. 101AC.
26 Germanus, *De haeresibus et synodis*. PG 98, 80A.
27 See Chapter 8. Commonly enough, the ground for a defective christology is a deficient metaphysics which has failed to grasp that 'with the idea of God as creator, as source of *esse* (roughly, the being of the thing not just over against a world-without-it, but over against *nothing*, not even 'logical space') comes the idea of God as relevant to things precisely in virtue of transcendence. . . . This God must be at the heart of every being, continually sustaining his creation over against nothing as a singer sustains her song over against silence.' (H. McCabe O.P., 'The Myth of God Incarnate', *NB* (August 1977), p. 355).
28 John Damascene, *On the Holy Images* I. 16, PG 94, 1245AC.
29 Ib. I. 36. PG 94, 1264.
30 Ib., III.12. PG 94, 1333.

167

31 Ib., I.9–13. PG 94, 1243C–1244A.
32 Ib., I. 11; PG 94, 1241A. II.5; PG 94, 1288B. III.2; PG 94, 1320C.
33 Ib., I. 19. PG 94, 1249CD. I. P. Sheldon-Williams noted too the strongly Dionysian quality of much of John Damascene's teaching. 'The relation of image to archetype is equivalent to (Dionysian) participation, the relation of the lower to the higher order of a hierarchy', art. cit., p. 507.
34 See for instance, E. E. Evans-Pritchard, *Nuer Religion* (Oxford 1956), and from a very different school within the discipline, C. Lévi-Strauss, *Structural Anthropology* (New York 1963).
35 Nicephorus, *Antirrheticus* I, 30. PG 100, 277D–280A.
36 Ib.,III, 38–9. PG 100, 449CD.
37 Ib., I, 20. PG 100, 2448C. On Nicephorus' work see P. J. Alexander, *The Patriarch Nicephorus of Constantinople: Ecclesiastical Policy and Image Worship in the Byzantine Empire* (Oxford 1958).
38 Theodore, *Letters* II, 194. PG 99, 1589D.
39 Theodore, *Antirrheticus* I, 7. PG 99, 336D.
40 Ib.
41 P. Henry, art. cit., p. 24.
42 *Vita Theodori Studitae* 33–4. PG 99, 280C–4C.
43 P. Henry, art. cit.
44 A. M. Allchin, 'Creation, Incarnation, Inspiration', *Sob.* 4,6 (1962). Now also in *The World is a Wedding* (London 1978), p. 132.

Chapter 6: The Shape of the Artwork
1 See the conclusion to Chapter 3.
2 M. Wiles, *The Making of Christian Doctrine* (Cambridge 1967), p. 173.
3 M. Heidegger, *Being and Time* (London 1962), pp. 58–62.
4 H. Osborne, *Aesthetics and Art Theory*, pp. 96–113.
5 A. J. Ayer, *Language, Truth and Logic* (London 1936), p. 113.
6 W. Charlton, *Aesthetics* (London 1970), p. 17.
7 A. Kenny, *Action Emotion and Will* (London 1963), p. 129.
8 M. Dufrenne, *The Phenomenology of Aesthetic Experience* (Evanston 1973), p. xii.
9 Collingwood's view, set forth in *The Principles of Art* (London 1938) and deriving from the Italian Idealist aesthetician B. Croce, holds that the artwork is essentially an inner state of the artist, an intuition or 'expression'. This inner condition may be externalized into a public form, the 'artifact' of the (mental) artwork. Collingwood's aesthetics are criticized by R. Wollheim in *Art and Its Objects* (New York 1968): 'It is more plausible to believe that the painter thinks in images of paint or the sculptor in images of metal just because these, independently, are the media of art; his thinking presupposes that certain activities in the external world such as charging canvas with paint or

168

welding have already become the accredited processes of art. In other words there would not be Crocean "intuitions" unless there were, first, physical works of art.'

10 J. Maritain, *Art and Scholasticism* (London 1947).
11 M. C. Beardsley, *Aesthetics* (New York 1958), pp. 351–3 on art as a system of signs.
12 C. Ernst, O.P., *The Theology of Grace* (Cork 1974), p. 68.
13 P. Sherrard, 'The Art of the Icon', *Sob.* IV. 6 (1962).
14 G. Mathew, O.P., *Byzantine Aesthetics* (London 1963), pp. 106–7.
15 E. Trubetskoy, *Icons: Theology in Colours* (New York 1973).
16 R. MacMullen, *The World of Marc Chagall* (London 1968).
17 W. Haftmann, *The Mind and Work of Paul Klee* (London 1954).
18 Ib., p. 37
19 V. Miesel, ed., *Voices of German Expressionism* (New York 1970), p. 87, cited in R. Rosenblum, *Modern Painting and the Northern Romantic Tradition* (London 1975).
20 W. Haftmann, op. cit. pp. 191–205.
21 M. Dufrenne, op.cit. p. 378.
22 Paul Evdokimov, *L'Orthodoxie* (Neuchâtel 1959), p. 219.
23 M. Dufrenne, op. cit, p. 103.
24 J. F. Frary, 'The Logic of Icons', *Sob.* (Winter 1972).
25 J.P. Manigne, O.P., 'Entre masque et vision', *La Vie Spirituelle* 582 (1971).
26 H.-G. Gadamer, *Truth and Method* (London 1975), p. 63.
27 I. Murdoch, *The Bell* (Harmondsworth 1962), pp. 190–1.
28 I. Murdoch, 'The Idea of Perfection' in *The Sovereignty of Good* (London 1970), p. 40.
29 Ib., p. 66.
30 Ib., p. 65.
31 Ib., p. 88.
32 I follow here J. Meyers, *Painting and the Novel* (Manchester 1975), who points out that the correspondence between art and fiction 'concerns the widest implications of perspective – the way an author shapes his vision of the world and enforces his way of seeing on the reader', pp. 1–2.
33 D. H. Lawrence, *Phoenix* (London 1936), p. 460.
34 D. H. Lawrence, *The Rainbow* (Harmondsworth 1949), p. 182.
35 T. H. Billington, *The Icon and the Axe* (London 1966), p. 38.
36 H.-G. Gadamer, op.cit. p. 101.
37 Ib., pp. 126–9.

Chapter 7: The Artwork and Christian Revelation

1   A. Dulles, *Revelation Theology* (London 1970).
2   A. T. Hanson, *Grace and Truth*, op. cit., p. 20.
3   E. Schillebeeckx, O.P., *Revelation and Theology* (London 1967), pp.

155–6.

4 Ib., pp. 156–7.

5 As Austin Farrer remarks, 'The events by themselves are not revelation, for they do not by themselves reveal the divine work which is accomplished in them; the martyrdom of a virtuous Rabbi and his miraculous return are not of themselves the redemption of the world' (*The Glass of Vision* (London 1948), p. 43).

6 Ib., p. 40.

7 Ib., p. 44.

8 Ib., p. 42.

9 Ib., p. 47.

10 This would be the approach of St Thomas, for whom revelation is communicated in prophetic knowledge. This form of knowing amounts to a supernatural gift of representations (sensory, imaginative, or intellectual) accompanied by an illumination of the judgement, thus enabling the mind to understand and exploit them. See *Summa Theologiae* IIa IIae 171–4 and *De Veritate* 12. The comments of a student of St Thomas who is also a biblical exegete may be found in P. Benoit, O.P., *Inspiration and the Bible* (London 1965), *Prophecy and Inspiration* (New York 1961), and 'Révélation et Inspiration selon la Bible, chez St. Thomas et dans les discussion modernes', *Revue Biblique* 70 (1963), pp. 321–70.

11 This conception was pioneered by Dom Odo Casel. See for instance his *The Mystery of Christian Worship* (London 1962) where he writes: 'What is the difference between the mystery of Christ and the mystery of worship? According to the letters of St Paul, the first is the reality of Christ himself: God, revealed in his Son made man; the revelation of himself which reaches its climax in the sacrificial death and glory of Christ. the Lord. The mystery of worship, on the other hand, is the presentation and renewal of that first mystery, in worship. By it we are given the opportunity of entering personally into the mystery of Christ. The mystery of worship, therefore, is a means whereby the Christian lives the mystery of Christ. . . . It is faith which gazes beyond the symbols at God's higher world as we experience it in the christian mysteries. . . . Christ himself became visible, and when his human form was taken away we became able to see him in the visible signs of his mysteries' (pp. 100–3).

12 In Thomist terms, man has a natural desire for the supernatural. This shows itself in his not being determined to any finite object as the goal and terminus of his existence. St Thomas' teaching in this respect was disengaged from the accretions of later interpreters by H. de Lubac, S. J., *The Mystery of the Supernatural* (London 1967), and *Augustinianism and Modern Theology* (London 1969).

13 J. Maréchal, S. J., *Studies in the Psychology of the Mystics* (London 1925); *Le Point de Départ de la Métaphysique* (Louvain 1922–6).

14 H. U. von Balthasar, *Love Alone: the Way of Revelation* (London

1968), p. 42.
15 P. Schoonenberg, S. J., *The Christ* (London 1972), pp. 32–8.
16 H. U. von Balthasar, op.cit., p. 43.
17 G. W. H. Lampe and K. J. Woolcombe, *Essays on Typology* (London 1957), p. 26.
18 A. C. Charity, *Events and their Afterlife* (Cambridge 1966), p. 80.
19 See above, Chapter 6.
20 Ib.
21 John 14.9.
22 H. McCabe, O. P., *The New Creation* (London 1964), p. 2.
23 For an exposition of our knowledge of God as mediated yet direct see Dom Illtyd Trethowan, *The Basis of Belief* (London 1961), pp. 67–8.
24 H. D. Lewis, 'Revelation and Art', *Proceedings of the Aristotelean Society*, Supplementary Volume 23 (1949), p. 7.
25 H. D. Lewis, *Our Experience of God* (London 1959), p. 203.
26 J. Moltmann, *Theology and Joy* (London 1973).
27 H. U. von Balthasar, *Verbum Caro: Skizzen zur Theologie* I (Einsiedeln 1960). 'Offenbarung und Schönheit'.

Chapter 8: Sketch for a Christology of the Image

1   Mark 10.32.
2   See Chapter 6.
3   See Chapter 7.
4   A. T. Hanson, *Grace and Truth*, op. cit., p. 26.
5   1 Cor. 2.6–10.
6   A. T. Hanson, *Jesus Christ in the Old Testament* (London 1965), pp. 141–4.
7   J. M. Robinson, *A New Quest of the Historical Jesus* (London 1959).
8   C. F. D. Moule, *The Origin of Christology* (Cambridge 1977), p. 3.
9   F. D. Dillistone, *The Christian Understanding of Atonement* (Welwyn 1968), p. 270.
10 Ib.
11 Especially Luke 23.24 and 43.
12 E. Stauffer, *New Testament Theology* (London 1955), pp. 25–9.
13 See Chapter 2.
14 A. T. Hanson, *Grace and Truth*, op.cit., p. 10.
15 From the enormous bibliography on this, see especially O. Cullmann, *The Christology of the New Testament* (London 1959) and F. Hahn, *The Titles of Jesus in Christology* (London 1969).
16 C. H. Dodd, *The Apostolic Preaching and its Developments* (London 1936); *According to the Scriptures* (London 1952).
17 See Chapter 4.
18 H. U. von Balthasar, *Herrlichkeit* (Einsiedeln 1961–), III.2,2, pp. 221–355. This encyclopaedic work is summarized in *Love Alone: the Way of Revelation*, op.cit.

171

19 John 1.14.
20 H. U. von Balthasar, *Love Alone: the Way of Revelation*, op.cit., p. 45; *Herrlichkeit*, op.cit., I, 1, pp. 22–3.
21 See Chapter 6.
22 K. Rahner, S. J., 'The eternal significance of the humanity of Jesus for our relationship with God', *Theological Investigations* (London 1963–), III. pp. 35–47.
23 1 John 1. 1–4.
24 John 9. 35–8.
25 A. T. Hanson, *Grace and Truth*, op. cit., p. 101.
26 J. Martyn, *History and Theology in the Fourth Gospel* (New York 1968), *passim*.
27 C. F. D. Moule, *The Origin of Christology*, op.cit., pp. 175–6.
28 H. Bettenson, *Documents of the Christian Church* (2nd edn, London 1963), p. 73.
29 K. Rahner, 'Current Problems in Christology', *Theological Investigations*, op. cit., I, p. 149.
30 J.-J. Latour, 'Imago Dei invisibilis' in H. Bouëssé and J.-J. Latour, ed., *Problèmes actuels de Christologie* (Bruges 1964), pp. 227–65.
31 See Chapter 2.
32 Georges Florovsky has spoken of the essential asymmetry in all sound christology. On the one hand, only God can save, while humanity's role is to co-operate in being saved. On the other hand, this asymmetry does not prevent Jesus from being fully man in all his activities but rather brings his manhood to a fully saved or healed completeness. See J. Meyendorff, *Byzantine Theology* (London 1975), p. 40.
33 See Chapter 4.
34 J. Galot, S. J., *La Personne du Christ* (Gembloux 1969), p. 179, cited by E. L. Mascall, *Theology and the Gospel of Christ* (London 1977), p. 167.
35 E. Yarnold, S. J., *The Second Gift* (Slough 1974), pp. 66–7.
36 K. Rahner, op. cit., pp. 43–4.

Chapter 9: The Eyes of Faith

1 H. U. von Balthasar, *Herrlichkeit*, op. cit., I, pp. 30, 111, 118.
2 M. Dufrenne, op.cit., p. 406.
3 P. Sherrard, art. cit.
4 See Chapter 3.
5 Compare, for instance, Gregory of Nyssa's remark that 'He who is beyond all knowledge and all intellectual grasp, the one who cannot be spoken, in order to remake in you the image of God has himself become, in his love for men, the image of the invisible God.' (*De perfectione christiana*. PG 46, 269).
6 H. Bouillard, *La logique de la foi* (Paris 1964), p. 34.
7 J. Mouroux,, *L'expérience chrétienne* (Paris 1952), pp. 50–1.

8   Augustine, *De Trinitate* XIV. 12,5. PL 42, 1048. On Augustine's doc-
    trine of the image see particularly G. B. Ladner, *The Idea of Reform*
    (Cambridge, Massachusetts, 1959), pp. 185–203. On the relevant parts
    of the *De Trinitate* useful comments may be found in M. Schmaus, *Die
    psychologische Trinitätslehre des heiligen Augustins* (Münster 1927),
    and E. Gilson, *The Christian Philosophy of St Augustine* (New York
    1960).
9   Augustine, *Confessions* X. 27. PL 32, 7954.
10 Augustine, *De Trinitate* XIV. 16, 22. PL 42, 1053.
11 On the Augustinian influence on St Thomas in this matter see the texts
    cited in the *sed contra* of the *Summa Theologiae* Ia. 93 and J. E.
    Sullivan, O.P., *The Image of God* (Dubuque 1963), ch. 6, 'St Augustine
    and St Thomas Aquinas'. On the monastic background of St Thomas
    S. Tugwell, O.P. has written:
    'It is . . . the monks who show us how St Thomas is using *ratio*. He is
    not inviting us to a purely 'rationalist' view of man, but picking up a
    theme that can be traced from Athanasius to Bernard and William of
    St Thierry. "Nature" is, for them, that which God created us to be,
    that which Christ enables us once again to be. In becoming "rational"
    man finds the harmony there was always supposed to be between the
    various elements in his personality and between him and his world.
    And it is an integral part of the deal that this restored humanity should
    be docile to something higher than itself, and this takes place through
    supernatural charity. Due to the indestructible Image of God within
    him, man can never be satisfied or fully happy until, through charity,
    he transcends himself and comes face to face with God. St Thomas can
    state far more clearly than his monastic precursors just how this heals
    and transforms man, and all the social, moral and ascetical implications
    of it; but the vision implied in his teaching is essentially that of the
    monks. It is their experience of life, their aspiration, for which he
    provides the scholastic theory, and his analysis only makes human
    sense against the background of their lives, their spirituality.' 'The Old
    Wine is Good', *NB* (December 1972), pp. 558–63.
12 R. Javelet, *Image et ressemblance au douzième siècle* (Paris 1967), I,
    p. ix.
13 Ib., p. xiii.
14 On William see J.-M. Déchanet, O.S.B., *William of St Thierry, The
    Man and his Work* (Spencer, Massachusetts, 1972).
15 William of St. Thierry, *De natura et dignitate amoris.* PL 184, 382C.
16 Ib., PL 184, 382D.
17 William of St Thierry, *De natura corporis et animae.* PL 180, 721CD.
18 William of St Thierry, *De natura et dignitate amoris.* PL 184, 396D.
19 William of St Thierry, *Meditationes orativae* 8, 7. PL 180, 232A.
20 William of St Thierry, *Letter* 271.
21 William of St Thierry, *Spedulum fidei.* PL 180, 385A.
22 Ib.

23 Ib., PL 180, 386CD.
24 J.-M. Déchanet, ed., *Exposition sur la Cantique des Cantiques*, SC 82 (Paris 1962), p. 24.
25 William of St Thierry, *Speculum Fidei*, PL 180, 393C. On the theme of the play of vision and likeness see L. Malavez, 'La doctrine de l'image et de la connaissance mystique chez Guillaume de St-Thierry', *Recherches de Science religieuse*, XXII (1952).
26 William of St Thierry, *Speculum Fidei*, PL 180, 393C.
27 William of St Thierry, *Super Canticum Canticorum*, 1. PL 180, 473C.
28 Song of Songs 1. 7.
29 William of St Thierry, *Super Canticum Canticorum* 64–5. PL 180, 494A–D.
30 Ib., 19. PL 180, 479A.
31 Ib., 83. PL 180, 505C–D.
32 Ib., 94, PL 180, 505C–D.
33 On this see J.-M. Déchanet, 'Amor ipse intellectus est. La doctrine de l'amour-intellection chez Guillaume de Saint-Thierry', *Revue du moyen âge latin* 1 (1945). More generally, see M. Scheler, *The Nature and Forms of Sympathy* (London 1954) for an account by a philosopher of the phenomenological school.
34 Odo Brooke, O.S.B., 'Towards a theory of connatural knowledge', *Cîteaux*, 4 (1967).
35 William of St Thierry, *Super Canticum Canticorum* 17–18. PL 180, 478D–479A.
36 U. Simon, 'The Multidimensional Picture of Jesus', in M. Hooker, and C. Hickling, ed., *What about the New Testament?* (London 1975), pp. 116–26.
37 Ib.
38 H. McCabe, O. P., 'The Incarnation: an exchange', *NB* (December 1977), pp. 550–1.
39 E. Trocmé, *Jesus and his Contemporaries* (London 1973), p. 25; cf. W. Kasper, *Jesus the Christ* (London 1976), p. 68.

Appendix: On Models and Metaphors

1 G. F. R. Lloyd, *Polarity and Analogy* (Cambridge 1966), pp. 384–420.
2 P. Wheelwright, *The Burning Fountain* (Bloomington 1968), pp. 3–31.
3 I. G. Barbour, *Myths, Models and Paradigms* (London 1974), p. 6.
4 A. Farrer, *The Glass of Vision*, op.cit., p. 148, where he writes, 'Poetry and divine inspiration have this in common, that both are projected in images which cannot be decoded, but must be allowed to signify what they signify of the reality beyond them.'
5 F. Ferré, 'Mapping the Logic of Models in Science and Theology', *The Christian Scholar*, 46 (1963), p. 31.
6 E. Nagel, *The Structure of Science* (London 1961).
7 Barbour, op. cit., ch. 4.

8   I. A. Richards, *The Philosophy of Rhetoric* (New York 1936), p. 94.

9   P. Wheelwright, *Metaphor and Reality* (Bloomington 1962).

10 The model should be used only for purposes it is suited to, just as we would not use a Mercator projection map to compare the areas of Taiwan and Tobago, nor an equal areas map to find out the correct shape of Tahiti.

11 I. Ramsey, *Models and Mystery* (Oxford 1964), p. 61. See also his *Religious Language* (London 1957), pp. 49–89. Ramsey remarks that 'Other disciplines will be judged primarily on the quality of their articulation; theology will be judged primarily on its ability to point to mystery.' This is no doubt ultimately true, but the adverb 'ultimately' must be allowed its full weight.

Index

177

Kasper, W., 175
Kenny, A., 169
Kierkegaard, S., 29, 148, 160
Kitzinger, E., 163
Klee, P., 96–8
Kleist, H. von, 97

Ladner, G. B., 61, 165, 173
Lambert, W. G., 179
Lampe, G. W. H., 113, 171
Latour, J.-J., 132, 172
Lawrence, D. H., 102–3, 170
Lawson, J., 165
Legge, J., 163
Le Guillou, M. J., 166
Leo III, 76, 78, 82
Leo IV, 81
Leo V, 81–2
Leontius of Neapolis, 58, 164
Leuuw, G. van der, 18–19, 159
Lévi-Strauss, C., 168
Lewis, H., 116–17, 171
Leys, R., 165
Lindsay, J., 158
Lloyd, G. F. R., 175
Lossky, V., 24, 160
Lubac, H. de, 165, 171
Lubin, A. J., 159

McCabe, H., 116, 168, 171, 175
McMullen, R., 169
Malraux, A., 6, 158
Mango, C., 78, 167
Manigne, J. P., 169
Maréchal, J., 110, 171
Maritain, J., 169
Martin, R. P., 162
Martyn, J., 172
Mascall, E. L., 173
Mathew, G., 94, 169
Mauser, U., 159, 160
Maximus Confessor, 53, 72–4, 126, 166, 167
Mayer, A., 165
Meer, F. van der, 52, 163
Meyers, J., 170
Michael III, 82

Miesel, V., 169
Mill, J. S., 91
Millet, J. F., 11
Moltmann, J., 117, 171
Monet, C., 9, 10, 11
Moore, G. F., 161
Moore, H., 138
Moule, C. F. D., 121–2, 171
Mouroux, J., 140, 173
Munch, E., 127
Murdoch, I., 100–1, 169
Murray, Sr. C., 50, 55, 163
Mussner, F., 162

Nagel, E., 175
Newman, J. H., 51
Nicephorus of Constantinople, 82, 85–6, 98, 167, 168

Orbe, A., 165
Origen, 63, 64–5, 66, 68, 74, 142, 149, 165
Osborne, H., 158, 169
Ostrogorsky, G., 77, 82, 167

Pamphilus, 65
Paulinus of Nola, 56, 164
Pedersen, J., 159
Pelikan, J., 76, 167
Perkins, A., 161
Peter Abelard, 142
Philo, 27, 46, 162
Philostorgus, 56, 164
Pisanello, 97
Pissarro, C., 9, 11, 158
Pitra, J. B. F., 166
Plato, 101, 153
Pool, P., 158
Pseudo-Athanasius, 164

Rad, G. von, 159, 160, 161
Rahner, K., 128, 132, 172, 173
Ramsey, I., 157, 175
Read, H., 12
Rembrandt, 140
Renan, E., 50, 163
Richard of St Victor, 142